Leading through the Quagmire

Ethical Foundations, Critical Methods, and Practical Applications for School Leadership

Ernestine K. Enomoto
Bruce H. Kramer

Rowman & Littlefield Education
Lanham, Maryland • Toronto • Plymouth, UK
2007

Published in the United States of America
by Rowman & Littlefield Education
A Division of Rowman & Littlefield Publishers, Inc.
A wholly owned subsidary of
The Rowman & Littlefield Publishing Group, Inc.
4501 Forbes Boulevard, Suite 200, Lanham, Maryland 20706
www.rowmaneducation.com

Estover Road
Plymouth PL6 7PY
United Kingdom

British Library Cataloguing in Publication Information Available

Library of Congress Cataloging-in-Publication Data
Enomoto, Ernestine, 1949–
   Leading through the quagmire : ethical foundations, critical methods,
and practical applications for school leadership / Ernestine K. Enomoto,
Bruce H. Kramer.
      p. cm.
   Includes bibliographical references and index.
   ISBN-13: 978-1-57886-555-0 (hardcover : alk. paper)
   ISBN-13: 978-1-57886-556-7 (pbk. : alk. paper)
   ISBN-10: 1-57886-555-7 (hardcover : alk. paper)
   ISBN-10: 1-57886-556-5 (pbk. : alk. paper)
   1. Educational leadership—Moral and ethical aspects—United States.
   2. School administrators—Professional ethics—United States. I. Kramer,
Bruce H., 1956– II. Title.
   LB1779.E66 2007
   174'.9378—dc22   2006035408

∞™ The paper used in this publication meets the minimum requirements of
American National Standard for Information Sciences—Permanence of
Paper for Printed Library Materials, ANSI/NISO Z39.48-1992.
Manufactured in the United States of America.

Contents

Foreword v
Robert J. Starratt

Acknowledgments ix

Introduction xi

Part I: Foundations

1 Ethical Foundations 3

2 Ethical Tension, Judgment, and Consequences 19

3 Religion and Religious Attitudes 41

4 Feminist Ethics and Beyond 55

Part II: Methods

5 John Dewey and Democratic Leadership 73

6 An Inquiry Method for Working Ethical Dilemmas 89

Part III: Applications

7 Cases to Consider 109

8 Teaching Ethical Deliberation 131

References 145

Index 151

Foreword

I read this book wearing several hats, and I suggest it would be an important book for any audience wearing one or another of these hats. First and foremost it will be useful for any professor who is teaching, or planning to teach, a course in ethics for aspiring or actual educational administrators. I also found it helpful for my own scholarly development as a scholar who writes about ethical leadership. As a professor in a school of education, I encounter practitioners in the field who are dealing with multiple ethical issues embedded in their daily practice and am asked to help them work through some of the stickier ones, and from that perspective, this book is also helpful. Finally, though I do not wear the hat of superintendent of schools, I would suggest that this book would be useful for that audience of educators, first to refresh their own ethical understanding and practice, but also as a potentially useful book to discuss, chapter by chapter, over a series of monthly seminars with their principals. This exercise would be especially helpful since the authors argue, rightfully, that dealing with ethical issues requires a consistent method that in turn should be learned by everyone in the system, all the way down to the students themselves.

This book distinguishes itself from other books on the topic of ethical leadership. Among other things, I would pick out the following:

- It rather courageously includes a topic ignored, or poorly treated, in some texts, namely the connection between religious belief and ethics.

- It provides a generous treatment of feminist ethics that not only aids understanding of that important social development but also blends that perspective into and enriches their method for addressing ethical issues facing administrators.
- It clearly posits the democratic social context as the diverse yet pragmatic source of values for ethical decision making.
- It provides a clear method for ethical decision making that goes beyond rationalistic, either-or, computational decision making to bring in
  - the desires and ideals of the people involved;
  - a search for a common *enough* good to get people to compromise; and
  - expectations of an imperfect and temporary decision that, while a genuine response to the immediate problem, is understood as a moment in a developing history of these specific people facing these specific circumstances who tomorrow will probably adjust and refashion another temporary advance.

This is a book by two professors who have struggled with their pedagogy and with the design of learning experiences in their courses. They teach in different contexts—one in a Catholic university, the other in a state university. They use differing pedagogies—one more socratically provocative, the other more of a stage director who coaxes out student self-understanding and cognitive clarification through debate and role playing. One is a male, the other a female. These differences can appeal to a broad audience who can find in the range of the authors' dissimilarities possibilities for crafting their own pedagogy.

They share, however, a strong commitment to a democratic leadership approach to creating a community of ethical decision makers who teach one another in the process of using a common method for ethical deliberation. That method is exploratory (attempting to describe fully what is actually at stake); dynamic (the method is not a one-dimensional sequence of logical deductions but rather flows with the evolving process of constructing, deconstructing, and reconstructing a rich understanding of the situation); imaginative (besides exploring the duties called into play, it involves imagining various responses that might improve the whole context of the problem); and capacity building (the use of the method strengthens participants' capacity for moral deliberation and moral action). I will leave it to the reader to discover the power of this method. Let me only say that I find their method the most helpful one I have seen in the various treatments of ethical decision making in the recent literature on the topic.

The core strength of this book, I believe, is its balance. The authors provide a clear presentation of foundational theories and show how each perspective can be used to counterbalance the exclusive use of one perspective. This generous-enough treatment of the more traditional approaches is brought into dialogue with more critical theories, especially through a refreshing exposition of feminist ethics. The authors then go on to frame the whole ethical context and a sophisticated method for responding to ethical dilemmas through an updated version of Dewey's democratic landscape in dialogue with eco-feminism's sensitivity to the social ecology of ethical challenges. This balance throughout the book does not result in bland, watered-downed generalities, but rather in a deeper and stronger leadership approach to ethical decision making that is clearly in line with much of the best literature on distributed leadership. I believe that this volume will become one of the most helpful books available for courses in ethical leadership in administrative preparation programs.

Robert J. Starratt, professor of education
Boston College

Acknowledgments

Our partnership began with a mutual interest in teaching ethics and in the challenge of adequately conveying how to engage in ethical deliberation. The idea for writing this book occurred as we proposed how we might work with our students. Bringing our different yet complementary ideas together, we were able to build on a proposal for inquiry and for ultimately democratic ethics in leadership. We thank Tom Koerner for believing that this would be a worthwhile endeavor, and university colleagues like Jerry Starratt, Don LaMagdeleine, Bob Paull, and Carolyn Carr who have encouraged our efforts along the way.

At the University of Hawaii, Ernestine Enomoto worked with colleagues who read drafts and helped to clarify her thinking. Thanks go to Ann Bayer, Barbara DeBaryshe, Cecily Ornelles, Tracy Trevorrow, and Lois Yamauchi for encouragement and support in the writing process. Ernestine especially values the thoughtful comments on the religion chapter by mentor and friend Mitchell Ratner.

At the University of St. Thomas, Bruce Kramer has taught two courses in ethics, one for school administrators and one for doctoral students. He is indebted to his coteacher, Deb DeMeester, with whom he has agonized over readings and activities to develop students' ethical decision making. This past year, he tried out chapters in various forms with his classes, seeking feedback and guidance from his students. While they are too many to mention here, he is grateful to all for their honesty. These courses have provided the grist for the mill upon which this book is based.

Finally, we would like to thank our families for their unwavering commitment to us individually. We thank Misao Enomoto and Evelyn Emerson for being there for us always.

Introduction

It may not seem like much of a problem. The district policy clearly states that possession of any weapon or weaponlike toy on the school premises is an automatic expulsion. The school board and superintendent support the policy 100%. So why does the principal, Karen Lee, feel so torn by what has happened? Noni, a student in her school, had been found carrying a small toy gun in her backpack. Not a gun-toting youngster, she is a six-year-old kindergartner who recently emigrated from Mexico. She does not speak much English, and Karen suspects that neither do her parents. The plastic toy gun was a prize won at the neighborhood store. Did Noni even know it was a "weaponlike toy"? The principal feels caught between her duty to uphold the policy and her desire to consider the circumstances of the situation. To this day, Karen wonders if she did the right thing, both for Noni and the school.

The incident did happen, as do so many similar kinds of incidents in classrooms and schoolyards across the country. School leaders are called upon to make judgments where the rules are clear, but the rules don't seem to take into account the finer points of the situation. As you read Karen's predicament, you may have reacted quite differently than she did. Perhaps you feel that there should be leniency for a six-year-old ESL student. Or perhaps you feel that rules are rules, and as unfortunate as it is, Noni must be expelled because those are the consequences for her action. Karen felt pulled by the circumstances of Noni's age and language. But school district policies do not differentiate for age or English comprehension. As principal, Karen has a duty to those rules and toward protecting those who are in her care. Here is an ethical dilemma, a judgment to make between what is the right action and what good might result.

Negotiating these kinds of dilemmas is what this book is about. It is about acquiring an ethical understanding to work through situations like Karen's in a reflective, discerning manner. It is about recognizing that ethical tensions that arise from the perceptions one has of one's duty, of the outcomes that are best for all, and of the personal and professional values deemed most important. This book is about accounting for individual differences and the effect of one's unique background such as social class, race-ethnicity, gender, religion, or culture, while at the same time considering our shared values and beliefs that unify us as a society. It is also about critiquing individual experiences and challenging habitual responses that fail to address the situation at hand. All of these aspects relate to becoming democratic leaders who must make ethical decisions in increasingly diversified settings.

ASSUMPTIONS OF THIS BOOK

If ethics is central to school leadership, then three assumptions need to be stated up front. First, we define *ethics* as philosopher William Frankena (1963) does, as that which is intended to be helpful in answering questions about what is right, good, or obligatory. Ethical judgments can be about a specific situation—for instance, "What Noni did was wrong"—or they can be general in nature—for instance, "All students should have the right to a quality education." As school leaders, we would likely make judgments about what we should do as well as what others might do, what is deemed just or caring action, what should be tolerated, and so on. Additionally, we want to be able to analyze and critique our reasoning and judgments. This is called metaethical thinking, which examines the meaning of our actions and reasoning for them.

Second, we assume that all decisions, regardless of how small, have an ethical component. Even the simple administrative task of assigning lockers or establishing a master schedule can pose ethical dilemmas for educators. These decisions are judgments to be rendered based upon personal, professional, and communal values and beliefs. There will be intended and unintended consequences affecting students, their families, faculty, staff, and the community at large. For these reasons, all decisions, whether consciously or unconsciously made, can be interpreted as applied ethics.

Third, we assume that our role as school leaders is to care for the needs of the young people placed in our charge. Our duty is to serve all students fairly, equitably, and respectfully while negotiating diverse needs and different options available to them. How might educators ensure consistent high-quality teaching and learning for all those enrolled in our schools? How can schools provide for those with greater needs than others? What about balancing the demands made by varied community groups? In answering these questions, we recognize that there is no one best system that fits all. For those who lead schools and school systems, the challenge includes understanding one's context as well as one's personal and professional values.

Proceeding on these three assumptions, we consider how leaders might make ethical judgments about individual desires and needs while taking into account the groups these individuals represent. How do leaders act ethically for their schools or for the system as a whole? To answer this question, we draw upon John Dewey's notion of democratic leadership and propose that democracy is an appropriate metaethic for action as well as for critiquing our actions. We introduce an inquiry method to guide ethical deliberation and conflict resolution. Such a method allows for understanding the current context of schools along with the habitual responses that might stymie action. It also calls for more creative problem solving followed by reflective discernment once action has been taken. We propose that working ethical dilemmas by using this inquiry method creates a more responsive and caring place of learning in our schools.

WHAT WE INTEND AND WHAT GUIDES OUR WRITING

Our intent in this book is to provide a combination of philosophical grounding and practical application using a democratic approach to ethical deliberation and decision making. We are not prescribing the exact outcomes or right processes in your specific case because we believe that leadership is contextual. That is, it must account for the particular individuals, issues, and challenges of the given situation, so that a one-size-fits-all solution probably will not suffice. But we do offer a set of guidelines to direct your thinking in your particular situation.

One of these guidelines was discussed above—the idea that democratic leadership is fundamental to do the work required of school administrators. A democratic approach strives to honor individual differences and be inclusive of the multiplicity of perspectives held. It at the same time negotiates for the good of all. It attempts to address the demands of diverse individuals while under the constraints of uniformity and standards-based education. We hope to demonstrate how a democratic approach to leadership can be a workable model for resolving conflicts and negotiating ethical dilemmas.

Another guideline that informs this book is that inquiry and reflection are critical in decision making. In making sound ethical judgments, leaders need to investigate problems fully and comprehensively. As much as possible, we believe that they need to be open to information from all sources, communicating with the parties involved in the situation. They need to be able to reflect thoughtfully on intended actions and consequences. We propose a method that supports doing the necessary inquiry and reflection demanded of school leaders.

A third guideline is the idea of "working the dilemma," rather than resolving it. To paraphrase Dewey, resolving a situation does not mean that disparate viewpoints do not exist. Tensions between individuals will remain, waxing and waning as time progresses and as the situation evolves. This idea of "working the dilemma" is preferable because it allows leaders to see the larger whole, one that cannot be totally controlled. Peter Vaill (1996) likens leading to being in permanent white water going down river rapids. We are not in control, but we can learn to control our own responses and reflect upon actions to be taken. This metaphor views leadership as the raft that will get us through the rapids. We see leaders as ensuring that ethical deliberation and judgment take place in school. Further, we believe that democratic leadership must be in the context of a moral imperative for schools.

Moral Imperative for Schools

Michael Fullan (2003) describes the moral imperative for schools in this way. Moral purpose in leading a public education institution means "having a system where all students learn, the gap between high and low performance becomes greatly reduced, and what people learn enables them to be successful citizens and workers in a morally-based knowledge society" (p. 29). It is not sufficient that a school administrator manages competently, maintains good public relations, and sustains high student achievement. Much more is demanded from the leadership. "At the school level . . . the moral imperative of the principal involves leading deep cultural change that mobilizes the passion and commitment of teachers, parents, and others to improve the learning of all students, including closing the achievement gap" (p. 41).

This means looking beyond the technical and managerial solutions toward one's responsibilities to others as well as to the school (Sergiovanni, 1992, 1995). For example, administrators can assist in creating specific conditions of practice to address the needs of diverse students. They can provide care for the well-being of individual students and their families (Beck, 1994; Noddings, 2003). They can encourage inclusive teaching and learning, and they can explore ways that culturally relevant teaching practices can be enacted (Riehl, 2000). But more than considering strategies to deliver outcomes, administrators can engage with others in the work of schooling. They need to take responsibility for delivering authentic learning and relevant practices that build citizens for a democracy (Starratt, 2004). It is this work that designates school leaders to be "moral agents" different from those of other institutions (Greenfield, 1993).

The moral imperative for education extends beyond the school. According to Fullan (2003), leaders at regional and national levels need to be encouraged to help each other and work collaboratively. This is exemplified in what Fullan calls "a culture of shared commitment across the district" (p. 52). Consider what it might be like for a principal whose school is placed on the watch list to have all administrators in the district offer to give support and assistance. Rather than going it alone, that principal would be able to tap into the shared commitment of the entire district. Riehl (2000) also suggests that school administrators build school community connections that extend into local communities. Schools can be mobilized into the process of community development and provide services to strengthen communities (Strike, 2006). Here is a much broader vision of what the moral imperative might be beyond schools and districts, with implications for the future.

Leadership Preparation

In preparing prospective school leaders for their work, university faculties have stipulated that an examination of moral-ethical issues be included among course offerings. This contrasts with earlier administrative preparation programs of the 1970s, according to McCarthy (1999) who reviewed University Council of Educational Administration (UCEA) programs. She found that little attention was given to ethical issues in earlier programs, whereas by the 1990s, ethical issues and concerns had been either incorporated within traditional course offerings or were delivered in special seminars.

Surveying all UCEA member schools during that time, Beck and Murphy (1994) reported that nearly 60% of the respondents were concerned about providing learning opportunities dealing with ethics. In a subsequent study of UCEA members' mission statements, we found a supporting finding (Kramer, Paull, & Enomoto, 2002). Of the 40 statements available, 24 (60%) had statements that ranged from specific values to prescribed ethical action. Of those programs, 15 were specifically designated or titled "ethics," for example, EDU914, Ethics in Educational Leadership, at the University of Dayton. In the remaining 9, ethics was taught within other courses. For example, at the University of Maryland, a course in human resources featured ethical issues confronting managers. Often in more traditional courses, like Introduction to School Administration, a discussion of values, ethics, and morals was noted in the course catalog.

In the past decade, evidence suggests that more attention has been placed on issues of values and ethics, with more integration of the topic within coursework. Shapiro and Stefkovich (2005) indicate a broader perspective than one grounded primarily in the justice perspective (Strike, Haller, & Soltis, 1998). Other approaches include perspectives that embrace caring (Beck, 1994; Noddings, 2003); critique (Starratt, 2003); and combinations of both (Enomoto, 1997; Katz, Noddings, & Strike, 1999; Starratt, 2003).

Standards and Ethics

Standards for moral leadership have given further impetus to the study of ethics in the preparation of school leaders. In November 1996, the Interstate School Leaders Licensure Consortium (ISLLC) specified six national performance standards in school administrator preparation, identifying the knowledge, skills, and dispositions deemed necessary to be effective educational leaders (ISLLC, 1996). The Council of Chief State School Officers, representing state superintendents nationwide, adopted these ISLLC standards and encouraged other professional educational associations and agencies to do the same. The council also encouraged that similar standards be adopted by educational agencies and regulatory bodies within each state. According to Maxcy (2002), the ISLLC standards have been most influential in moving educational administration toward a standards-based model for administrator preparation.

Of the ISLLC standards, Standard Five relates specifically to ethics and leadership. It states, "A school administrator is an educational leader who promotes the success of all students by acting with integrity, fairness, and in an ethical manner" (Council of Chief State School Officers, 2001). In achieving this standard, a prospective school leader is expected to know and understand various ethical frameworks and professional codes of ethics in order to serve diverse school communities. Also important is knowledge of the values of one's specific community, coupled with an understanding of the diverse views held by its members. Within the national context, ISLLC Standard Five stipulates that an administrator be responsible for upholding the rights and beliefs of our country. It is expected that our school administrators understand and commit to providing for the common good while ensuring that every student receives a free, quality education.

According to the Standard Five performance indicators,

> The ethical administrator considers the impact of her administrative practices on others, uses the influence of the office to enhance the educational program rather than for personal gain, and expects that others in the school community will demonstrate integrity and exercise ethical behavior. (Council of Chief State School Officers, 2001)

Given the established ISLLC standard of ethics, and more course offerings addressing ethical issues, there is a clear need for prospective administrators to attend to ethical concerns in their decision making. How to engage in these issues and attempt to negotiate ethical dilemmas is what we present in this book.

OVERVIEW OF CONTENTS

The three main parts of this book are part I: Foundations (chapters 1–4), part II: Methods (chapters 5–6), and part III: Applications (chapters 7–8).

Part I: Foundations

The four chapters in this section provide a philosophical and conceptual grounding for thinking about moral-ethical leadership, democratic education, and inquiry-based methods. In chapter 1, we consider how school leaders make decisions. What is ethical decision making? What makes for an ethical judgment? Determining the bus schedule or filling a teacher vacancy could be seen as standard operating procedure or might be done in the same way year after year. However, each decision calls into question the administrator's choice and reasoning. From that general premise, we discuss how school administrators examine their decisions, acknowledging habitual choices and making conscious decisions that take various factors into account. We describe the Greek origins shaping our Western ethical thinking and the kinds of questions that we might ask in deciding what is right. We examine the needs, desires, and values of the individual and the group. Consideration is given to personal as well as professional ideology in decision making. In so doing, we propose considering democratic ethics and its implications for school leadership.

Chapter 2 presents four common sources of ethical tension that create conflict among individuals and groups. The first source, duty-based ethics, proposes ways to consider ethical conduct within one's personal and professional duties. Second, desires-based ethics (also known as ends or outcomes) focuses on what is deemed best for the majority. The third source of ethical tension emphasizes the individual's character and behavior (virtue ethics), which contrasts with the fourth source, the group or societal perspective on character and behavior. Grounded in Western philosophical language, each source can form an ethical system with assumptions and beliefs used in decision making. Conflicts arise when people operate from different ethical systems, and we illustrate this in the chapter. Judgments and consequences are part of our deliberation. We specify what can inform our judgments as well as how we might weigh consequences for actions.

In chapter 3, we explore the topic of religion and ethics. While it is often difficult to discuss religion and its influence on ethical decision making, we propose the need to address how our religious backgrounds might influence the antecedent beliefs forming our decisions. Beginning with a definition of religion, we consider how religious thinking has evolved and influenced our values and beliefs. We look at how our religious traditions vary. As well, we consider the freedom of religion allowed in our U.S. Constitution and practiced in American society. Beyond the legal dimension, we refer to Dewey's distinction between religion and religious attitude, which enables us to be more open to inquiry. We consider the work expected of administrators who need to honor religious freedom while accommodating diversity and multiple perspectives.

Extending the critique on predominant ways of thinking, chapter 4 on feminist ethics offers an alternative perspective that informs our moral-ethical decisions and is different from an ethic of justice and moral development. We take an in-depth look at feminist ethics, defining feminism and suggesting how it applies to ethical decision making as school administrators. With its limitations in mind, we close the chapter by suggesting how eco-feminism offers us a model of critique that is highly appropriate to democratic leadership.

Part II: Methods

In these two chapters, we specify a rationale and means to engage in ethical deliberation in a systematic way. In chapter 5, we present Dewey's ethic of democratic leadership as an effective means of engaging others and striving toward collaboration. We consider how leaders traditionally look at their work in contrast with how they might ethically view their roles and responsibilities. Dewey and Tufts (1932b) write,

> [Traditional leadership roles] encourage the idea that some "leader" is to show the way; others are to follow in imitation. It takes time to arouse minds from apathy and lethargy, to get them thinking for themselves, to share in making plans, to take part in their execution. But without active

cooperation both in forming aims and in carrying them out there is no possibility of a common good. (p. 347)

Thus, we propose an inquiry-based method that aims to be inclusive, contextual, democratic, and empirical. It asks leaders to subsume their individual desires and take others into account. We illustrate using an example of an administrator struggling with an ethical dilemma. Working through the example, we show how inquiry and facilitation might work, but in the next chapter we present a fuller description of the method.

Chapter 6 describes an inquiry-based approach for working through ethical dilemmas to arrive at decisions. It takes the reader sequentially through four phases of discernment and action. We also suggest collaborative decision making that can apply to public settings where many members need to be informed and make decisions collectively. Just as health care professionals consult ethics boards in reflecting about dilemmas, so too might schools and school systems consider how public discourse can be incorporated where ethical choices may be debated, exposed, examined, and enacted. Such collaborative inquiry and dialogue fulfill the democratic charge.

Part III: Applications

Chapter 7 presents specific cases for ethical deliberation and decision making. The reader may wish to select cases that are of particular interest. Each case is presented first in synopsis and then in greater detail. The case narrative identifies a problem or situation, reveals the participants' thinking, raises some key issues, and suggests possible implications. A general set of discussion questions applies the inquiry method, and more specific questions relate to the individual cases. While some cases are event specific, all suggest historical contexts that encourage the reader to dig deeper and probe more rigorously. Unlike case narratives that present problems and offer solutions, the reader is invited to consider personal as well as professional reactions and alternatives to the dilemmas. Our experience is that ethical dilemmas require working through an iterative process that will evolve as one's knowledge and skills increase.

Chapter 8 discusses teaching ethics. Beginning with our own teaching of ethical deliberation, we describe how we as individuals have approached teaching this topic and the inquiry method. We also share our commonalities as well as our differences as we have struggled to make sense of philosophical language in ways relevant to our students. Beyond the teaching of ethics in leadership preparation, we suggest that democratic ethics can be applied to the classroom and to the school. We extend this to the role of leader as teacher and specify how democratic ethics as a framework proposes a different style of leadership.

CONCLUSION

Both authors have been teaching ethics with practicing and potential school administrators for at least ten years. We actually developed our friendship first around the challenges we experienced in teaching ethics to those in leadership positions. What philosophical background would be beneficial and not overwhelming? How could the study of ethics be made relevant and meaningful? What examples might illustrate concepts like utilitarianism and secondary doubling? How could realistic cases be presented? What does it mean to engage in ethical deliberation? We have also found that students and practitioner friends struggle with personal as well as professional decisions. They wonder about whether their decisions are sound and whether they are right. They reflect that doing what is right and good might not be enough in dealing with diverse views and conflicting needs.

We wrote this book for them as well as for the many Karen Lees who serve as principals in our schools. It is our attempt to ground the discussions about what is the right thing to do in a framework using ethical language and logic. It is also about remaining open and inclusive as democratic practitioners leading diverse schools. By reading this book, we hope that you will gain a better understanding of how to think through ethical dilemmas and work toward resolving them well.

Part I

FOUNDATIONS

CHAPTER 1

Ethical Foundations

Leaders must ask "What is the right thing to do?" and "What good will result?" Asking questions about the process as well as the results, they can discriminate in order to make judgments on right action and good outcomes. In ethical language, the words *right* and *good* have specific meaning in terms of process (the "right" thing to do) and result (a "good" outcome). While it is hoped that leaders always seek right processes and good ends, the two aspects can be at odds with each other, particularly in complex situations. This is what we explore in this chapter by providing some basic concepts used in ethical judgment.

First, we set the context by describing the Greek origins of our Western ethical thinking and how this thinking has directed the kinds of questions that we have come to ask. Next, we discuss how individual and group needs may conflict and be more difficult to reconcile in ways that work for everyone. Third, we look specifically at the concepts of right actions and good ends, describing what they mean in terms of ethical decision making. Among the considerations are antecedent and consequential factors that may determine what is right and good. Finally, we propose what might be considered an ethical dilemma. All of these basic concepts lay the foundation for discussing moral leadership and democratic ethics.

GREEK ORIGINS

Ethics as characterized by Western ethical philosophy can be described as "the search for a rational understanding of the principles of human conduct" (Rowe, 1991, p. 121). What is meant by a good life? What is a good person, or for that matter a good society? How do we know what is right? What is considered to be virtuous? This line of questioning has dominated Western thinking, beginning with the ancient Greeks through to the present day. While contemporary issues and perspectives may differ somewhat from those of the Greeks, this line of thinking is still recognizable as descendent from the discussion and debate that took place in Greek city-states of the fifth and fourth centuries BCE.

Probably the most influential Greek philosophers from that period were Socrates, Plato, and Aristotle. Socrates (ca. 469–399 BCE), nick-named the Gadfly, was said to *sting* people into thinking clearly for themselves by asking probing questions that critiqued the Athenian way of life and its established social order. He was so critical of society that he was put on trial and later killed. But his aim was to raise people's awareness to a higher level, reflecting justice for all, including the least of society's members. After Socrates, the term *ethics* (in Greek, *ethos* or *ethike*) came to mean "questioning of the sacred customs" (Fasching & deChant, 2001, p. 15). A guiding tenet of his philosophy was that "a position is only as good as the arguments that support it." He cautioned against taking any proposition whatever as authoritative and criticized social customs and norms.

Despite this strong orientation toward criticism, Socrates held the view that humans have purpose or function (teleological view) and that they need to determine what that purpose is. Accordingly, virtue (in Greek, *arete*) was derived from this wisdom. Once known, humans could reason and would always know what was the right thing to do. Socrates was confident that if anyone did wrong, he or she had not thought enough about the matter. His belief in human reasoning was captured in the maxim "No one goes wrong deliberately."

Plato (ca. 427–347 BCE), Socrates' student, recorded dialogues from his teacher that reflected the Socratic approach of oral argument but in written form. Later, in his own work, *The Republic*, Plato developed ideas about the individual, the state, and morality that differed from but extended his teacher's tradition. Among these ideas was the notion that empirical knowledge (sensory perception) was filtered through human reasoning. Plato proposed that real knowledge, by contrast, was found as part of the structure of the universe and was unchanging. Mankind would need to "penetrate beyond the veil of appearances to the hidden, unchanging reality" in understanding the knowledge of goodness (Buckle, 1991, p. 162). For Plato, real knowledge was morality.

Aristotle (ca. 384–322 BCE) in turn was Plato's student and later became the tutor of Alexander the Great. While he agreed with Plato that human beings were "essentially social beings," he was more pragmatic and interested in "what ordinary people thought about morality on a day-to-day basis" (Robinson & Garratt, 2004, p. 40). In writing the *Nicomachean Ethics*, Aristotle provided a rational basis for the idea of goodness and justice that occurs from organizing a society in a harmonious way. There was legal justice that man created, and natural justice, "which everywhere has the same force and does not exist by people thinking this or that" (*Nicomachean Ethics*, vol. 7, as quoted in Buckle, 1991, p. 162).

Despite various critics over time, the Greek philosophy introduced by Socrates and developed by Plato and Aristotle remains a cornerstone of our Western ethical reasoning. Like those philosophers, we identify with the importance of human reasoning, the freedom to choose our individual actions, and the belief that it is possible to live peacefully with others. According to Rowe (1991), "The rise of Greek ethics can be seen in large part as a reflection of the overlaying of a fundamentally individualistic ethos with the demands for co-operative behavior implied by the political institutions of the city-state" (p. 127). These Greek philosophers believed that ultimately there was no conflict between the individual and the state. Moreover, they held to a belief that by using reason and engaging in argument and debate, we could arrive at knowing the right action to take.

THE INDIVIDUAL AND SOCIETY

As early as the fourth century CE, St. Augustine of Hippo (354–430) linked the Christian Gospel teachings with Plato's philosophy. He believed that as a result of Adam's fall from Eden, all people had an evil impulse and needed to be restrained by the power of the state and the laws of the church (Thompson, 2003, p. 63). His *Confessions* reflect the inner turmoil and struggles that he felt wrestling with God (Augustine,

1963). But he clearly saw a separate realm for the religious (the city of God) different from the secular (the city of man). The former was to be ruled by the church and its bishops, while the latter was governed by the political order represented by kings and emperors (Fasching & deChant, 2001, p. 58).

By the medieval period, St. Thomas Aquinas (1224–1274) argued for society's laws to be for the good of all and reflective of "natural law," which was God's providential ordering of the world (Thompson, 2003, p. 41). Individuals needed to be tempered and subjected by reason, governance, and divine rule. Aquinas declared, "The human will is subject to three orders. Firstly, to the order of its own reason, secondly to the others of human government, be it spiritual or temporal, and thirdly, it is subject to the universal order of Divine rule" (*Summa Theologiae, Ia, Iiae, q8, aI* as quoted in Haldane, 1991, p. 133). What he and other Christian theologians added to basically Greek philosophy was divine intervention and transformation of virtues into God's blessings.

In the 14th century, the intellectual and political worlds of Western Europe were transformed by the rise of empirical science, the fragmentation of the Church of Rome, and the Protestant Reformation. Attempting to retain their ground, Catholic scholars continued to expound on the works of Aquinas and Aristotle in response to the changing times. This was exemplified by the Dominicans, who advanced the argument for a "just war" and the legitimate use of violence to defend society. More current with the times was the philosophical movement to return to Platonic doctrines, promoting the idea of humanity and its moral value. This philosophy was later embodied in Renaissance humanism, which by the 15th and 16th centuries emphasized human accomplishments while minimizing God's role in them.

Since individuals needed to determine a right course of action, a study of ethics emerged. According to Midgley (1991), some thinkers believed that ethics was man's egoistic response to maximize good ends for himself while trying to live with others. Thomas Hobbes (1588–1679), a 17th-century English Royalist and philosopher, contended that human life was basically "solitary, poor, nasty, brutish and short." Left to their own devices, there would be social anarchy. Hobbes proposed that human beings needed to agree upon a "social contract" in order to be regulated and avoid conflicts with each other. "Everyone comes to agree to a legal agreement not to kill or steal from each other, because it's ultimately in everyone's interest" (Robinson & Garratt, 2004, p. 56). Like humanism, the notion of a contractual agreement established by men in society placed them at the center, not God or the Divine.

Contrasting with Hobbes's rather bleak view of mankind, Jean-Jacques Rousseau (1712–1778) espoused that humans were born as moral beings with the potential for goodness. In writing about a young man's education in *Emile*, Rousseau proposed educating children toward their innate goodness and not allowing their innocence to be corrupted. His writings spurred the Romantic movement, a return to the natural order of life and living harmoniously within it. American philosopher Henry David Thoreau (1817–1862) expressed this philosophy in writing *Walden*, which espoused a simpler, more natural way of life.

By the end of the 19th century, the simple natural life in America was rapidly being replaced by increasing urbanization, industrialization, and waves of immigration. At this point in our history, we agreed to put aside some of our self-interest for a greater social good. This was a significant development because social groups were made up of individuals who often had specific desires and needs that were not always compatible or complementary with each other. Putting aside individual interests was necessary if we were to live collectively, each surrendering something for the good of the whole. But how was this to be done?

Two different ethical philosophies emerged to answer this question. The first, utilitarianism, was introduced by English philosopher Jeremy Bentham (1748–1832). In *Principle of Utility*, he wrote that humans were either seeking out pleasure or avoiding pain. Thus, he argued, "Instead of relying on vague ideas about feelings or conscience, you classify and measure any action in terms of how many units of pain or pleasure it will produce" (Robinson & Garratt, 2004, p. 71). Judging actions based upon results, Bentham introduced the notion of "the general good," referring to the greatest happiness of the greatest number. He theorized that in any situation with moral choices, "the right thing to do is that which is likely to produce the greatest happiness for the greatest number of people" (Thompson, 2003, p. 67).

Similarly, John Stuart Mill (1806–1873) favored utilitarianism but proposed that it be made less materialistic by prioritizing cultural and spiritual kinds of happiness rather than only physical and sensual pleasures. Further, he believed that "morality should still be about obeying moral rules, even if the rules were decided upon Utilitarian grounds" (Thompson, 2003, p. 76). In his essay *On Liberty*, Mill wrote that as long as people did not interfere with the freedoms of others, they should be allowed to think and do as they pleased.

Different from utilitarianism was the ethical proposition advanced by the Prussian philosopher Immanuel Kant (1724–1804). In *Fundamental Principles of the Metaphysics of Morals* (1785), he proposed that moral action is done out of a sense of duty rather than as a result of following one's inclinations or desires, and such action is executed without regard for the consequences. That is, individuals act out of a personal sense of what is right. Given this duties-oriented (deontological) stance, Kant believed that "ethics is all about what these duties are, how we find out what they are, and why we must obey them" (Thompson, 2003, p. 81). Using reasoning, we could work out what to do by a test of universality, that is to say, by asking what would happen if everyone did the same thing and there were no exceptions. This became Kant's system of compulsory rules, or the "categorical imperative." More will be said about this in chapter 2.

Kant also believed that ordinary people could learn to apply abstract moral principles. While earlier philosophers did not believe that everyone possessed a methodical way of consciously using such principles, Kant held that morality could actually be used by all (Schneewind, 1991). This view of moral autonomy, that individuals were capable of seeing for themselves and deciding for the good of all, held a major place in the 19th and early 20th centuries.

Both ethical philosophies had their share of critics. G. W. F. Hegel (1770–1831) argued that the content of Kant's formal principle came from the institutions, vocabularies, and orientations of the society in which one lives, and thus it was not strictly an individual choice as Kant had proposed (Schneewind, 1991, p. 154). In a similar line of reasoning, Karl Marx (1818–1883) introduced the view that humans were the products of their social class and its related ideology (attitudes, values, and beliefs determined by an economic structure). He saw workers cut off from their labor and functioning in a process from which some other person reaped the profits. As laborers, they were subject to their employers and employment and thus could not be considered morally autonomous.

Another critic, French existentialist Jean-Paul Sartre (1905–1980) believed in the uniqueness of each human being. This view of moral philosophy, he argued, could not be derived from purpose (as Aristotle proposed), rationality (Kant), or pain versus pleasure (Bentham). "It is we ourselves who are responsible for our 'essential' natures or characters" (Robinson & Garratt, 2004, p. 98). For Sartre, morality was about the freedom to choose one's action. Drawing from Nietzschean views, Sartre argued that "morality rested on nothing but the totally untrammeled free decision of each individual," and each must make a "purely personal decision about it—and then, to be in good faith, live accordingly" (Schneewind, 1991, p. 155).

Regardless of whether we believe, as Sartre did, that individuals are personally responsible, or, as Marx and Hegel did, that social, political, and economic institutions dictate individual thinking and preempt morally autonomous action, the tensions between the individual and society continue to play out as we attempt to consider what is best for the majority (utilitarianism) and what duty might determine is the ethical thing to do (deontology).

RIGHT ACTION AND GOOD ENDS

In ethical language, the words *right* and *good* have specific meanings. *Right* refers to the process, way, or path of action. Its focus is on the means rather than the end. By contrast, the word *good* refers to the end result, product, or outcome of an action. This distinction should be retained in addressing ethical questions about what to do, why, and how to do so (Kramer, 2006b).

Throughout history, these two concepts have been defined and redefined within their historical and social context. For example, before the time of Socrates in fifth-century BCE Greece, *good* meant anything that the king was (e.g., wealthy and powerful) or did (e.g., conquered enemies, sired many children). Others could be wealthy or powerful, but since they were not the king, their good outcomes were not considered the same good as the king's. Later, the word *good* took on a more general meaning, not only whether things were associated with the king but rather how they affected other people.

Most leaders find themselves making decisions where they weigh what is good for individuals against what is good for the group as a whole. In the educational setting, consider classroom management. Teachers judge how much behavioral disruption they will tolerate before acting to control it. Is a child who is misbehaving better served by remaining in the classroom and participating with classmates? Or is the class becoming unruly and disrupting learning? Can this individual child's disruptive behavior be tolerated or not? As the leader of the class, the teacher considers the good of the individual child against the good for the class as a whole.

Likewise, school leaders weigh individual needs with group needs in judging good ends. As a principal, you may have encountered assertive parents advocating very effectively for their children, and you may have been persuaded by the arguments they made. But you also recognize that your obligation is to look beyond the individual needs of those children and consider all others in the classroom and the school. As principal, you might acknowledge that the child's needs, while being well served, are met at the expense of the other children in the school. Here, you are weighing the good for the many against the good for the one.

To further complicate matters, there may be varied individual needs conflicting with groups that may not necessarily be aligned. For example, a rural school superintendent was recently challenged with having to consolidate two eighth-grade classes at different schools into one middle school program. At one school, a group of parents objected to the bus commute that their youngsters would have; another group wanted to ensure that there was adequate coursework so that their children would have sufficient credits in preparation for high school. At the other school, some parents objected to the newcomers who came in as a result of the consolidation. Some parents liked the plan but not at the present time, seeking to postpone it until later. There were varying issues and concerns from school personnel as well as parents. The superintendent needed to hear their concerns as well as weigh what might be best for all in the long term as well as the short term. Politically, the superintendent was being pressed by the school board to enact a smooth transition as quickly as possible. The situation was multifaceted, with individual and group needs that varied and were conflicting.

Desired outcomes might also be attempted by unskillful or inappropriate means. If we consider the classroom management situation above, the teacher has several options to handle disruptive student behavior. But it is considered inappropriate to employ punitive or hurtful means to discipline a child. While a beating might result in a quiet child, the process would also produce potentially harmful consequences. In this respect, the way we get to a good end is as important as the outcome itself.

Right action and good ends are ethical concepts that focus on means and ends. But these two concepts are not mutually exclusive of each other. The ideal is to achieve good outcomes through right action. In practice, however, right action does not always yield the good that was intended. Later in this book, we will discuss how to consider right means and good ends in determining what action to take. But first we turn to what we need to consider in making judgments and to what causes angst in decision making.

ANTECEDENT FACTORS

Ethical judgments are based on a variety of factors relating to how we deliberate and make decisions. Basically, these factors can be classified in two ways, either as antecedent or consequential. Antecedent factors are those things that have occurred or exist before a decision is made, such as one's family background, education, religion, life experiences, peer influences, and so on. It is likely that an individual raised in a multiethnic working-class neighborhood would have different life experiences as compared with someone raised in a homogeneous rural community. These kinds of life experiences might affect how the individual thinks about language, cultural difference, and in turn education.

It is also possible that individuals sharing religious beliefs and practices might have a common ideological grounding regardless of their class, race-ethnicity, gender, or national origin. For instance, two

Catholics with different life experiences (e.g., a fifth-generation Polish American raised in Michigan and a recently emigrated Mexican American living in San Antonio) might share fundamental values and beliefs that shape their ethical judgments. Similarly, someone of minority background (e.g., a Puerto Rican American) might feel greater affinity toward another minority (e.g., a Vietnamese American) despite where they were raised or what their specific ethnic origins are because of their immigrant experiences assimilating into American society. These antecedent factors relate to an individual's personal values and beliefs that in turn affect ethical decision making.

Shaped by individual values, beliefs, and responsibilities, we have been taught both formally and experientially in ways that contribute to the assumptions that we bring to any given situation. Suppose that as a teacher, you had a run-in with your union representative, leaving you with a bad impression of teachers unions in general. As a consequence, it is quite possible that as a school administrator, you will interpret the motives and actions of the union representative in your building in a skeptical manner. If, on the other hand, your prior experiences with the union had been positive, you might tend to be more trusting and open to the union and its representatives.

Our prior experiences and beliefs can sometimes be so powerful that they do not allow us to see anything other than what we already "know." For example, if faculty and staff have come to believe that students always seek to take advantage of any rights they are granted, that strong belief might deter cultivating students' sense of autonomy and independence in the school. Assumptions that we hold individually and collectively play an important role in determining how open we are to new concepts. Moreover, Stephen Fesmire (2003) reminds us, "The feeling that something is good does not necessarily make it so, and the judgment that it is the good of this situation is a working hypothesis qualified by experimental confirmation or disconfirmation" (p. 97). As leaders making ethical decisions, it is very important to be aware of our assumptions in order to seeing differently and be more open to others' viewpoints.

Antecedent factors can also include the professional duties and responsibilities of being a school administrator. It is the administrator's professional duty to ensure that the youngsters attending her school are served well. It is also the administrator's responsibility to uphold the policies and procedures of her school, district, educational association, or organization. For example, in considering how to revise a student attendance policy, a school principal would need to take into account the existing policies for not only the school but the district and possibly the state. There might be regulations within one's professional educational organization that need to be regarded as antecedent to deciding what action to take.

Rules and regulations, usually in the guise of policy, are meant to offer guidance, and perhaps even governance, in situations where judgment takes place. Their role is to shift the judgment from the actual situation to the interpretation of the rule in the situation. For instance, in the case of alleged harassment, the rules are meant to clarify the phenomenon of harassment, to initiate the process for determining when a situation meets the definition of harassment, and to guide the action taken. This direction can be very comforting for leaders because it means that the actual decision is not whether the situation is harassment but rather whether the situation meets the policy definition of harassment. Policies can offer specific guidance in ethically tricky situations.

There might also be unwritten cultural norms within the day-to-day operations of the organization that are antecedent factors to be considered when making ethical decisions. School administrators, particularly those new to a school, may be unaware of organizational rituals, routines, and unspoken norms that affect the entire school. Consulting with those who are knowledgeable about the school's culture, traditions, and changes would be beneficial. For example, a 25-year veteran second-grade teacher may not be on the leadership team designated by the principal, but that teacher might exert a great deal of influence over the pace of change in her school. Perhaps the school secretary would be important to consult before making policy changes regarding parent involvement and business partnerships.

As with individual and group differences, personal and professional antecedents may not be aligned, causing ethical tensions to surface when deliberating what action to take and how to decide. How does one handle a decision where the professional expectations directly contradict one's personal beliefs or vice versa? For example, within the current standards and accountability climate, many educators feel conflicted over having to teach within narrowly defined achievement expectations measured by standardized tests. Professionally, they believe that they should be covering a much wider curriculum and be allowed more discretion to address their students' academic, social, emotional, and other needs. The educators' belief in a more holistic curriculum and adapted instruction conflicts with the directive that they must teach a specific curriculum and apply a reform model to meet annual yearly progress goals. Examining antecedent factors can suggest the kinds of values, beliefs, and assumptions held by individuals within the organization and the likely ethical tensions that might exist.

CONSEQUENTIAL FACTORS

The second category of factors to consider in decision making is what we either believe or know will happen once a judgment is rendered. What will result from this decision? Who will be affected, and how might they be impacted? How many individuals will benefit? Will anyone suffer from the action? Are there unintended as well as intended consequences from this action? What are some immediate short-term effects? Are there long-term consequences that should be factored into the decision making? Reflecting upon these kinds of questions is critical because we hope to make the best decision possible.

As our experiences broaden, we are better able to specify consequential factors. For example, a teacher's experiences might be limited to a particular classroom or grade level. With experiences as a grade-level chairperson or dean of students, that individual would gain a broader perspective to make decisions about what is best for students in the school. Given specific administrator training and mentoring, the individual might be better equipped to consider a fuller spectrum of consequences resulting from an administrative action. This is not to say that we necessarily make better decisions because of our position and purview as an administrator but that we are better prepared to think through the numerous consequences.

It should be noted that we bring all of our life experiences into the equation, not only our educational ones. That is, a teacher may be a soccer coach as well as a choral director. He or she might be a parent with several children, or be one of several siblings in the same town or spread across the country. These varied experiences enable the individual to consider consequences more broadly than someone with limited experiences in collaborating with others and coordinating group efforts.

As mentioned earlier, utilitarianism is a school of ethics that emphasizes the consequences for the majority. Philosophers also use the term *consequentialism* to designate this ethical system. It holds that happiness is the ultimate good and that the best acts are those that produce the greatest good for the greatest number. As such, it offers a quantifiable formula for determining what action should be taken. But as Kant noted, all situations do not necessarily fit. There are certain principles like freedom, justice, and equality that might preempt any consideration of majority or minority. Regardless of how many individuals benefit, a violation of these universal principles requires our attention.

At times, antecedent and consequential factors seem to fit with each other, where our life experiences together with our values and beliefs are aligned with the likely outcomes that we seek. Personal beliefs and professional expectations seem aligned consistently with each other toward goals that we can agree on. Our ideals are aligned sufficiently with our aims so that we can do what we believe to be right and strive toward outcomes that are desirable. However, as we collaborate with others, it is more likely that there will be clashes over varied values, beliefs, life experiences, and other factors. There may be individual needs that clash with group needs. Personal ideology might contradict professional expectations and result in opposition and unintended consequences. Such situations create ethical dilemmas, requiring us to look more closely, reflect thoughtfully, and demonstrate leadership.

ETHICAL DILEMMAS

What is a dilemma? Rushworth Kidder (1995) reminds us that a dilemma is when two or more options are equally viable choices. In essence, this means that we are looking at a situation where there might be several possible "right actions," or a good outcome might occur at the expense of right process or protocol. We acknowledge that leaders in schools often identify their dilemmas in terms of finding the lesser of two evils. The choice might be about forcefully suppressing all opposition in order to yield good or worthwhile outcomes. Or we might employ the right means to produce compromised results. Perhaps the choice will have some significantly negative consequences for some individuals while the majority benefit.

In any case, dilemmas require that leaders engage in careful analysis and discernment to arrive at ethical judgments. What antecedent factors, both personal and professional, need to be considered? What likely consequences might result from the actions taken? What means have been suggested to arrive at what ends? Have we weighed all the factors related to the decision? Have we sufficiently thought through the positives and negatives that might result from our actions? We will explore dilemmas more fully in chapter 6 as we describe an ethical method of inquiry for handling complex problems.

For now, it is enough to know that a dilemma exists when there are two or more equally valued choices in a situation. One path is taken at the expense of the other. That is, consequences will differ substantially depending upon the action taken. When it is a choice between two wrongs, then you will be faced with trying to mitigate any harm done by the choice made. This actually raises the question of whether an ethical leader should be considering any course of action that is "wrong." We think that the reality of leadership is such that leaders often have to stretch their ethics around the particular circumstances at hand. Badaracco (2006) states that this is about developing moral-ethical codes that are sufficiently

> complex, varied, and subtle as the situations in which they often find themselves . . . enables leaders to fully understand the complexities of the situations they face, to see them in the same terms as others do, and to communicate more powerfully and effectively. (pp. 33–34)

Discerning the sources of ethical tension in a dilemma is helpful in that it exposes the reasoning or logic that may be underlying the decision. Suppose you interpret a problem as being primarily a conflict among varied beliefs about education; then the strategies associated with working the problem will have to do with finding people's commonalities or deconstructing their beliefs and assumptions. If, on the other hand, you perceive that the problem relates to what is best for the majority, then you might work the problem by determining what is "best," who is "the majority," and what activities are associated with such a determination. In chapter 2, we will be speaking about various sources of ethical tension and how to identify and discern them.

DEMOCRATIC ETHICS

It should be very clear from this chapter that individuals hold values, beliefs, knowledge, and experiences that influence their choices in resolving ethical dilemmas. To demonstrate moral leadership in public education requires what we have come to call "democratic ethics." By this term, we do not mean political systems or political parties. It is not about distinguishing Democrats from Republicans, Blue States from Red States, or conservatives from liberals. Neither is it particularly about constitutional rights (e.g., freedom of speech, right to assembly and protest) or citizenship responsibilities (e.g., voting; paying taxes; abiding by national, state, and local laws).

Instead, we adhere to John Dewey's view that "democratic ethics" refers to how educators maximize the potential and growth of each person in the situation while ensuring that the groups to which individuals belong support their growth (Kramer, 2006a). This means that there is a synergy between individual and group, personal and professional, and means and ends. These aspects cannot be categorically separated from each other, because they are integral and affect each other.

In effect, we believe that moral leaders must find ways to exercise democratic means that fully consider individuals and their groups. When presented with an ethical dilemma, leaders need to involve as many people as possible in a democratic process, gathering input, involving those concerned, getting issues clarified, and negotiating a resolution that does not separate winners from losers. Leadership can promote democratic practices while negotiating the myriad of possible consequences that could result from an action. This can be a time for school organizations and their members to grow. Or, conversely, it can be a time when they are stymied and debilitated through formulaic or conditioned responses (LaMagdeleine & Kramer, 1998). We speak more about this in chapter 5, where we more fully describe democratic leadership, and in chapter 6, where we discuss a mode of ethical inquiry and how it might be applied to complex ethical dilemmas.

SUMMARY

In this chapter, we introduced the reader to key concepts related to ethics and ethical decision making. Tracing the Greek origins of our Western philosophy, we presented two different philosophies for resolving what actions to take. Utilitarianism proposes considering the "greatest happiness for all," while deontology advocates action done out of a sense of duty. In ethical language, we also distinguished that the word *right* refers to means, whereas *good* refers to end results. Our deliberation before making an ethical judgment requires us to consider antecedent as well as consequential factors that relate to individuals and groups. Notably, ethical dilemmas occur when two or more options are equally viable but pose conflicts among one's values and beliefs. These could be personal as well as professional values that conflict. By defining these concepts, we have presented a specific vocabulary forming the ethical systems, and we have introduced Dewey's democratic ethics used in decision making.

CHAPTER 2

Ethical Tension, Judgment, and Consequences

In an essay entitled *Law and Manners* (1924), English jurist John Fletcher Moulton placed ethics as the middle ground between the law, which required obedience, and total freedom of expression. He called ethics "obedience to the unenforceable," in which

> there is no law which inexorably determines our course of action, and yet we feel that we are not free to choose as we would. . . . It grades from a consciousness of a duty nearly as strong as positive law, to a feel that the matter is all but a question of personal choice. (Moulton as quoted in Kidder, 1995, p. 67)

Useful and pragmatic, this definition reminds us that ethics involves negotiating or deliberating a middle ground where there might not be a clear-cut choice. We may find ourselves deliberating between what we believe to be our duty and what we might prefer to do. Our choices may not be equal or necessarily desirable. Or we may find ourselves having to choose between values that are personally important and values that are sanctioned by our professional organization. Weighing these choices can create stress and tension as we decide what we ought to do.

In this chapter, we describe four commonly acknowledged sources of ethical tension and provide the philosophical language that forms ways of thinking about each source. Conflicts can arise when people operate from these different sources, and we illustrate how this can happen particularly in educational settings. We advocate that leaders need to understand these sources of ethical tension in order to negotiate workable resolutions and make reasoned judgments.

FOUR SOURCES OF ETHICAL TENSION

As an overview, figure 2.1 depicts the four sources of ethical action that can create conflicts as they clash with each other. The first source, *duties-based ethics*, is based upon law and rules. It is ethical thinking that comes from authority, such as religious precepts (e.g., the Ten Commandments, the Five Pillars of Islam) or government (e.g., the U.S. Constitution and the Bill of Rights). Such authority spells out the duties of a group member or citizen, that is to say, what a good person is responsible for doing in society. "At the heart of this morality is the idea of law which prescribes what is legitimate or obligatory" (Dewey, 1930, pp. 280–281). But this ethical system relates to more than what has been legislated or is legal; it aims at that which is governed by principles to be upheld by all regardless of consequences. It is called *deontological* or *universalist* ethics.

The second source, *desires-based ethics*, refers to those things that we desire or want. If we desire something, we probably believe that it would be "good" for us to have that something. For example, if we desire quality educational opportunities for ourselves, it is quite possible that we will believe that it would be good for everyone to have access to the same. But Dewey reminds us that what is good is relative, depending upon the historical context and subject to change based on the time, place, and circumstance of the situation. Using this logic, a desires-based system would be any type of ethical system based on the final outcome, because it is attempting to define an ultimate good end. For this reason, it is also known as *ends-based ethics*.

A third source of ethical tension arises as we consider individual characteristics or qualities of a person. It is identified as *virtue ethics*. Rather than consider one's duties or desires, we might ask what defines a "good person." What are the character traits or dispositions that they have or demonstrate? How do these traits relate to the decisions that they might make? These questions arise from the idea of virtuous persons and how they behave. Athenassoulis (2004) states, "Instead of asking what is the right act here and now, virtue ethics asks what kind of person should I be in order to get it right all the time." When we begin to discuss ethics from this viewpoint, we are considering a person's whole life and what makes for goodness. Virtue ethics, like trait theory, describes the qualities of a good person.

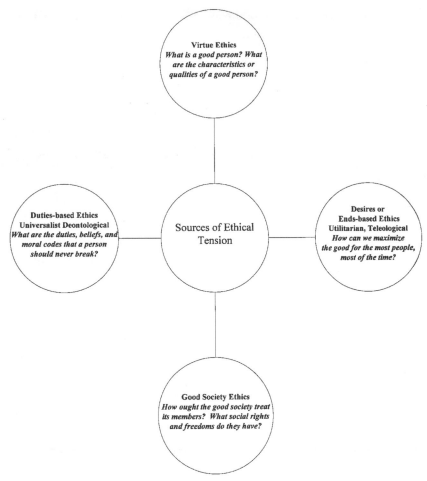

Figure 2.1.   Four Sources of Ethical Tension

The fourth source of ethical tension, *good society ethics*, recognizes that we do not live alone or isolated from others. Rather, we are part of an ever-widening circle of social groupings—our immediate and extended families, occupational groups, professional associations, sociocultural groups, religious affiliations, geographic collectives, and so on. Looking at these social groupings, we can readily see ethical qualities that define what might be considered good within the boundaries of those group affiliations. Conflicts arise when we as individuals differ from our group, as well as when we are torn between different groups' expectations. Good society ethics has us consider what is good for the group, the expectations of group membership, and the rights and responsibilities within the group and among groups within society.

In the next section of this chapter, we present the language and logic of each source of ethical tension in greater detail. We identify key philosophers who have informed the discussion about duties-based, desires-based, virtue, and good society ethics. We also show how conflicts occur among these four sources and where judgment comes into play in determining what action to take.

DUTIES-BASED ETHICS
(THE DEONTOLOGICAL/UNIVERSALIST SYSTEM)

When you think about duty, what do you consider? Do you think of your duties as a citizen or community member? Or perhaps you consider your obligations as an educator, school administrator, or professional. Perhaps you think first about your personal duties in your family as a spouse, parent, child, or sibling. Roles such as citizen, worker, professional, or family member have specific duties and responsibilities associated with them.

All duties can be defined by external and internal factors. For example, our affiliated groups (e.g., professional organizations, political affiliations, social clubs, church denominations) define the roles and responsibilities of their members. These would be considered external factors, different from how we ourselves might interpret those roles and responsibilities, which are internal factors. Further, duties can be thought of as either obligatory or privilege. To what extent does the word *duty* imply an obligation or burden when considering the responsibility to fulfill it? Conversely, do you consider the duty an honor or privilege? Both obligation and privilege might determine how we think of our duty and fulfill our responsibilities.

Ethicists draw from the Greek word *deon* (duty) to name deontological or duties-based ethics. Those who operate from this ethical system often have very strong beliefs coupled with a sense of responsibility and commitment to meet the expectations prescribed by their duties. Such strength of conviction can result in strong action, for example, demonstrating religious zeal or political activism on issues such as quality of life, the environment, war, poverty, and social engagement. In the world of duties-based ethics, belief spawns a sense of duty, and duty spawns behavioral action. Prussian philosopher Immanuel Kant (1724–1804) helped us make the connection among these three aspects—belief, duty, and behavior.

Duties-based ethics is probably best encapsulated in Kant's work, *Fundamental Principles of the Metaphysics of Morals*, published in 1785. In it, he proposed that a moral action was done out of a sense of duty rather than by following one's inclinations or desires. Such action was taken without regard for outcomes. For Kant, ethics was a rational application of reason, and reason should be able to lead to moral precepts (or maxims, as he called them). Using reason, one could work out what ought to be done. We specifically use the terms *belief* and *behavior* here because Kant saw ethical duty as an expression of intent, coming from inside the person.

He distinguished ethical duty from juridical (legal) duty, in which we are externally constrained by legal consequences. Ethical duty is that which we do because it fulfills our beliefs about what we ought to do. Consider two individuals who drive within the speed limit. One might do so believing that it is an ethical duty ("I ought to follow the speed limit to be a safe driver"), whereas the other individual drives at the speed limit because she does not wish to be ticketed. According to Kant's way of thinking, intent and belief determine which of the two drivers might be more likely to speed.

By separating ethical from legal arguments, Kant was able to describe what we ought to do all the time, not based on some external rule that was imposed, but on something inherent, namely that which we believe to be good. The task then was to determine moral precepts that were universal and could be applied to all. These were what Kant called imperatives meant for everyone to follow.

Further, he argued that our ethical aims were of a higher order than legal ones because legal aims were for controlling our behaviors within a given time and place. For example, some schools have dress codes that do not allow students to wear any jewelry, hats, bandannas, or other accessories. Do all schools have such restrictions? Is wearing certain clothing a universal duty for every student in every school? No, these restrictions are contextually specific and therefore are not universal. If a student goes to a different school, he must abide by the dress code of that school.

What, then, makes a moral precept a "universal" imperative? Kant distinguished two types of imperatives—hypothetical and categorical. Hypothetical imperatives are formulated as contingencies, such as "If you don't want to get a speeding ticket, then you should not drive in excess of the speed limit." Another hypothetical imperative is "You should only wear clothing prescribed by the dress code if you don't want to get sent to the office." By contrast, categorical imperatives imply actions taken always and everywhere and are therefore universally applicable.

> "Act according to a maxim which can be adopted at the same time as a universal law." Categorical Imperative is a moral rule without exceptions, and we are not to be concerned with the possible unintended consequences of such an application. (MacIntyre, 1966, p. 194)

We must follow this type of imperative, and it must apply to everyone, everywhere, and at all times. For example, suppose you adopted the categorical imperative to treat others with dignity and respect. Underlying such an imperative is the belief that other people have dignity and should be respected, and you also would believe that every person can and should treat others with respect to exhibit dignity. To test whether this is a categorical imperative, consider its negation. Could you treat someone poorly because they treated you poorly? Or could you treat people with dignity only if and when you felt like it? If that were the case, then no one could trust that dignity and respect would be present in human relations. This imperative would not meet Kant's test for being universally applied.

Another example of a categorical imperative is Kant's admonishment that humans should be treated as ends, not as means. That is, humans should always be treated with respect, and we should not use other people for our own gain. Such an imperative is typical of Kant, who believed in human dignity and expounded on this belief in his writing. It is the reason why many current philosophers and ethicists feel a kinship with him today.

However, there are numerous criticisms raised against Kant's thinking. The basic test of whether we operate morally is that we do our duty to the categorical imperatives we hold. According to MacIntyre (1966), Kant paid no attention to either context or consequences when assessing these imperatives. Without regarding possible consequences or analyzing actions taken congruent to those beliefs, a person might be inclined to rigid conformity to the categorical imperative. For example, suppose a friend provided you with classified information and asked that you protect his privacy by not disclosing the source. If an officer of the law demanded that you reveal the source of your information, Kant's system of compulsory rules would not allow you to lie. In this case, you would not be able to keep your informant's confidentiality and tell the truth at the same time.

Another criticism is that while Kant speaks about acting "out of duty," we do not necessarily know what someone else's maxims are. For instance, in business dealings, we would not be able to distinguish a person who is genuinely honest from a reluctantly honest person "who deals fairly only out of desire for a good business reputation and would cheat if a sale opportunity arose" (O'Neill, 1991, p. 177). The behaviors of the two persons would be the same, while the motivation and intentions might differ. As such, we look to the outward signs of conformity to maxims of duty, rather than what might have motivated that action.

The most common charge against Kant's ethics was made by Hegel, Marx, and others who alleged that a categorical imperative is "empty, trivial, or purely formal, and identifies no principles of duty" (O'Neill, 1991, p. 181). Hegel pointed out that Kant's moral law needed content and that such content was socially determined by the community in which a person lived. Moreover, the community might have a structure and impetus of its own that extends beyond individual choices. Issuing a similar critique, Marx suggested that more significant than individual choices and principles were the inevitable historical developments generated by economic forces.

Despite these criticisms, duties-based ethics remains an important consideration in leadership decisions because of the internal, deeply seated beliefs that people hold, as well as because of the responsibilities that people perceive to be part of whatever role they are playing. Conflicts often occur because people operate from what they believe to be their ethical duty in fulfilling their roles and responsibilities.

Suppose that as school principal, you are trying to lead your faculty through revising the math curriculum. But faculty members hold varied viewpoints about what is best for teaching mathematics; what textbooks, assessments, and technology to use; and how best to deliver such a curriculum. At one end of the math-beliefs spectrum are those who strongly believe that a traditional math program is essential for the students of your school. The beliefs they hold about right and good, teaching and learning, form a categorical imperative that they believe everyone should follow. At the other end of the math-beliefs spectrum are those teachers who believe that using an integrated math program will inspire more students, push the talented ones to do better, and keep the less talented ones engaged. Their beliefs make up a categorical imperative opposite to the first group of teachers.

Which group is correct? Each group of teachers holds strong beliefs shaped by their educational background and experiences. Both sides are acting according to what they believe to be the best way of meeting the needs of their students. Their entrenchment in these beliefs might make it almost impossible to adopt any curriculum that the entire school can agree upon and implement. Leading the faculty as a whole, you might feel paralyzed to make any change, but as school leader, you feel obligated to make changes. Forced into action, you declare, "The math teachers can't seem to come to any agreement, so I will make the final decision about the new math curriculum." Your action could alienate one group, disenfranchise the faculty, or undermine any school reform.

This example illustrates how differences in beliefs about duty and their associated categorical imperatives are a source of ethical tension. As a leader, you need to attend to the varied beliefs, values, and related senses of duty among your school members if conflicts are to be prevented and workable solutions made. Not paying attention to the categorical imperatives that others carry can result in the leader suffering the consequences of these deeply held beliefs.

DESIRES-BASED ETHICS
(THE TELEOLOGICAL/UTILITARIAN SYSTEM)

As noted earlier, desires relate to what we seek or want as a result of our actions. Ethicists refer to the Greek *telos* (end) and call this ethical system teleological or ends based. It is also known as utilitarianism as devised by the English philosopher Jeremy Bentham (1748–1832). In writing *The Principle of Utility*, Bentham argued that actions should be judged on the results achieved, as summarized in the phrase "the best for the most." Quite simply, utilitarians seek to maximize desired ends for the majority of people. Given a situation with moral choices, they would argue that "the right thing to do is that which is likely to produce the greatest happiness for the greatest number of people" (Thompson, 2003, p. 67).

What makes teleological ethics so attractive to decision makers? First, there is a sense of caring that comes with this reasoning. Considering individual's needs can seem very caring indeed. After all, don't we appreciate another person's consideration of our own particular situation? Focusing on what is "best for the most" implies that we care about maximizing positive outcomes for most of the people. We look for a positive outcome for most of the group, demonstrating that we care for the well-being of the group as well as for the individuals in the group.

Second, this ethical system offers a practical principle for leaders to do what is best for the majority of their constituents. Its rationale goes along with the democratic notion that the majority rules. The logic is easy to understand and justify. Acting according to the desires of the majority can feel like the most efficacious way, and possibly the most politically safe way, to lead a diverse group of people.

Here is an example of how desires-based ethics might work. A business is trying to decide what kind of health care should be offered to employees. As CEO, you know that most of your employees are young, fit, and generally healthy. Suppose that you could negotiate an employee health plan based on this fact. You also could save each of your employees a great deal of money by placing a low cap on the amount of health care dollars that the plan is required to cover each year. Perhaps you could even take the savings in health insurance and either reduce liability for insurance or offer an enhanced retirement plan. Taking such action would be considered very utilitarian. It is mutually advantageous for the company and the employees, and it seems to represent what is best for the most. Even if one of the employees needs more than what is covered in the insurance, it still meets the utilitarian standard of "best for the most."

But here is the limitation with this ethical system. Suppose one of your employees is diagnosed with a treatable but very long and expensive illness. The plan might not afford the coverage necessary, or that individual might incur a tremendous expense to be treated. Here, the needs of the one are not considered in the equation. Would it be right that the rest of the employees are able to save money at the expense of one employee's ability to get full coverage? Most of us recognize that our health situation could change at a moment's notice. The employee who is robustly healthy one day but in serious need the next will not be served if the utilitarian standard is applied.

How do utilitarian ethicists answer the questions raised by the example above? Bentham argued that by maximizing that which brings the greatest good to the greatest number, we are actually serving society as a whole. The rationale is very useful for policy makers who seek to maximize collective impact, but what about those in the minority? The health care problem above could be mitigated by asking, "Isn't it better for all of us to prepare for more care than we probably need at this time?" Such thinking is mutually advantageous to the employees who would be covered for the singly unpredictable health event, as well as to the company with its employees satisfied with the benefits received. It might even benefit the insurance provider with more money up front to invest and be ready for the company's more significant health care needs.

There are other critiques of desires-based ethics. If we follow this system of ethics to its logical end, then we might only look out for our own best interests. That is, we would want to make sure that our interests were aligned with those of the majority. But suppose our views were different from the majority. Could we support a minority point of view? To what extent could we consider the needs and desires of those with little power and influence? These are questions that raise issues with majority-rules logic.

A second critique is that desires-based ethics is extremely dependent upon an analysis of consequences for its value judgments. If we were only interested in consequences, then what about the universal imperatives that we value and believe in? Do we want to operate in a world that is so consequentialist that good cannot be determined until after the fact? While consequences should be considered in ethical decision making, we would be skeptical if there were no allowance for duty and universal principles. Overreliance on consequences in desires-based ethics also raises questions about "what is good?" and "who determines it?"

Finally, this kind of utilitarian thinking is susceptible to a contingency analysis, which poses "What if . . . ?" questions. While important to consider, we need to keep in mind that what looks like the best option for the majority right now might not be or might change over time.

CONTRASTING DUTIES WITH DESIRES

Before taking action in a situation, a leader needs to pay attention to what people believe (duties) as well as what they want to achieve (desires). This is not to say that individuals will not rise above their personal desires to fulfill their responsibilities, but there are times when one's perceived duties may conflict with another's most ardent desires in such a way that it is impossible to see any convergence of possible action.

Take for example the recently enacted federal "No Child Left Behind" laws, requiring that all children meet minimum standards of learning. Most educators may agree that this is a desirable end. Most may even commit to that duty as part of being a professional educator. However, suppose you are working with children whose lives are so fragile that just getting them to school seems to be an accomplishment. More than 20% of our children in the United States live in poverty, and many educators, while agreeing with the ultimate goal of No Child Left Behind, feel that it is paramount to take care of the physical and emotional needs of the children who experience such external variables. The desire to comfort and provide safety may come first, thus conflicting directly with the duty to meet academic standards. Add the obligation that the school demonstrate having made student achievement gains each year in order to avoid being restructured for missing Annual Yearly Progress (AYP) goals. The legal and ethical consequences may force school leaders to weigh what would be the best approach to ensure quality education for all children within the school or system.

VIRTUE ETHICS

In chapter 1, we discussed right actions (process) and good ends (out-comes). We asked, what is the right thing to do? As well, we needed to consider the good that was the aim. Both duties-based and desires-based ethics require that actions taken be judged as right or wrong. But there are other equally important ethical questions. For example, is it possible to know the actual goodness of a person? Should we have some way of judging a person's character, not just because they meet their responsibilities or maximize the good for the majority? In essence, we are asking, what does it mean to be a good person?

To answer such questions, ethicists have relied upon Greek philosophers Plato (ca. 428–354 BCE) and Aristotle (ca. 384–322 BCE) who attempted to define ethics associated with questions about what makes a person moral or good. This system of ethics became known as virtue ethics. A virtuous citizen of Plato's time was one who ful-filled his (emphasis on the masculine) role in the society, be he slave or master. Regardless of his role, the citizen was expected to be the best that he could be. Such role fulfillment was deemed to be a demonstration of good character. In contemporary times as well, we generally view individuals who fulfill their roles and responsibilities as being virtuous. However, could a thief or a criminal be considered "virtuous" if he is the "best" in his role? Considering particular ways of living and acting, ethicists needed to look beyond individual char-acteristics or qualities.

Plato's student, Aristotle, went so far as to discuss habits of ethical behavior that could be reasoned out. Plato felt that in order for a man to learn to discern the ethical, he would need to study the sciences and math. Aristotle strongly disagreed and believed that experience com-bined with the right beliefs would result in ethical wisdom. Virtue was an elaborate set of calculations based upon an ideal person, for which Aristotle gave a mathematical quality. He defined it as the midpoint be-tween two nonvirtues—one of excess and the other of deficiency—known as the doctrine of the means (Rowe, 1991, p. 128). For exam-ple, the virtue of prudence exists between the deficiency of miserliness and the excess of the spendthrift. Similarly, courage exists at the mid-point between recklessness and cowardice.

Perhaps the most significant modern virtue ethicist is Alasdair Mac-Intyre who, influenced by the writings of Aristotle, advocated a return to virtues as a way of connecting with what was historically considered "good." In addition, virtues help sustain practices that are consistent with those good ends. MacIntyre (1984) believed that virtues help keep the good traditions of a society intact while weeding out practices that are antithetical to social norms. "Lack of justice, lack of truthfulness, lack of courage, lack of the relevant intellectual virtues—these corrupt traditions, just as they do those institutions and practices which derive their life from the traditions of which they are the contemporary embodiments" (p. 223). For MacIntyre, the modern tendency to avoid calling some characteristic "good" has resulted in a lack of clarity in ethical language and a disturbing lack of social unity in terms of identifying those moral equivalents to which we should aspire.

In leadership, we often see virtue ethics in the guise of trait theory, which attempts to describe the good leader with particular traits. For instance, we see the leader as having character traits such as strength, determination, commitment, courage, caring, and so on, which are used to assess the leader's capability and decision making.

This is often evident in the process of selecting a new principal or superintendent. While the announcement for an administrator specifies necessary requirements and lists the responsibilities of the job, the selection committee might discuss the various candidates based upon their perceived virtues. For instance, in reviewing applicants, a committee member might comment, "Even though (the candidate) doesn't have a lot of experience, I felt his honesty would make him a successful leader." Someone else might identify another desirable trait. "Her references attest to her caring for the faculty and staff. That is the kind of leader we need here." The selection committee might base its final choice upon speculation about character traits (e.g., honesty, caring) rather than upon the applicant's capabilities and competence.

Virtue ethics is probably most visible when a person's character is called into question. Suppose that a leader is seen as trustworthy and loyal. She probably developed her reputation based on her dedication to the group that she serves and her willingness to follow through on what she says she will do. By contrast, another leader who is not trusted may have earned this attribution because of an inconsistent application of policies and procedures, a haphazard interpretation of the rules, or a lack of follow-through. We often base our work preferences more on the character of the individual than on her relative competence. This can be particularly problematic when we associate certain traits with general characteristics such as one's social class, race-ethnicity, gender, age, family background, religion, or the like.

This system of ethics allows us to move away from the duties-versus-desires reasoning found in ethical decision making. In virtue ethics, our actions are based upon what good people should do. Take the idea that good people should make good friends. They do things for each other based upon friendship, not upon whether they get something out of the relationship. They act out of caring toward their friends rather than because of benefits accrued. Such a belief is grounded in the qualities that exist long before any action is taken. This is one of the strengths of virtue ethics.

GOOD SOCIETY ETHICS

Usually ethicists discuss "good society" ethics by describing groups and their relationship with individual members. Specifically, what should an individual expect from the groups to which he or she belongs? What should the group expect from the individual? To answer these questions, a good group is often described in virtuelike terms. For instance, a good group might be just, fair, caring, productive, and so on, which are features of the group. For our purposes, we begin with the definition that a group is a social construct—individuals linked by common interest or affiliation. The "good" group then should maximize the abilities of its members to meet those common interests. But how is this done? Let's look at the concern for personal and mutual safety.

Suppose you live in a residential community and would like to ensure the safety of yourself and your family. To meet these requirements, you agree to a social contract with the larger community that involves giving up something to remain safe. You might give up free time in order to patrol the neighborhood and ensure that a steady watch is maintained. Alternatively, you might agree to pay into a common fund for hiring someone to watch over the community. This is what cities and counties do by employing police or security officers to patrol and protect our neighborhoods. Whatever the choice, you have given up something in order that the group as a whole may benefit. This contractual arrangement with the group will regulate action, avoid conflict, and provide for the safety of all who live in the community.

Consider another example of a social contract. As an educator, you are a member of a teachers union and must pay dues. While you may not like paying union dues, the membership enables you to have collective bargaining over individual negotiations in terms of pay, benefits, and working conditions. Union membership also offers you protection from being treated in an unseemly or unfair manner by a superior. The union would intervene on your behalf in such cases. It would ensure that due process is followed, provide for mediation, and advocate for your rights. In this instance, the good group fulfills its contract with its members (e.g., providing collective bargaining and protecting rights), and a good individual member fulfills a responsibility to the group (e.g., paying union dues). Notice the reciprocity between a good individual and a good group.

However, it is possible to use the same reasoning to justify a so-called prison state. The society offers safety and protection but only if the individual members agree to give up so many rights that their existence in it becomes oppressive. It is precisely this type of ethical problem that contemporary philosopher John Rawls (1971) sought to resolve. He proposed a means to determine a good society that would account for individuals being self-interested and yet willing to participate in a social contract that might benefit others.

What would cause a person to act for the good of the whole rather than based exclusively on self-interest? Rawls proposed this hypothetical situation. Individuals could design an ideal society, revising the laws accordingly, but they were to operate under what he called "a veil of ignorance." That is, they were required to construct the society without knowing where they would be placed in the resulting social order. They would not know their age, race, color, wealth, or social position. They would have no reference to any special interest group. In this situation, Rawls posited that rational people would wish the best for the least in society because under the "veil of ignorance," they might be at the bottom of the social order.

Accordingly, such a society would be "good" because it met two criteria. First, every individual would have the right to the greatest liberty possible. Second, social and economic inequalities would be justifiable only if they benefited those who were socially or economically disadvantaged. These criteria have been used to justify freedom of the press and progressive tax systems. In establishing social contracts on this basis, Rawls argued that there would be a balance between the rights of the individual and the needs of the society.

Critics of Rawls cite the hypothetical nature of the veil of ignorance. Based upon a fictional situation, they argue that Rawls' proposition appears to be unrealistic and useless. Even Rawls admits that other principles besides self-interest might govern how individuals decide to distribute resources, share benefits, or suffer consequences (Kymlicka, 1991). However, his position is useful in that he defines a good individual and can link the contractual arrangement between the good individual and the good society. Moreover, his premise that each person matters and is entitled to equal consideration is one that we endorse in our American democracy.

CONTRASTING VIRTUE AND GOOD SOCIETY ETHICS

Attempting to apply virtue ethics to the good society, there is an assumption that good people will necessarily build a good society. While it might be argued that good people will influence the society in which they are members, describing the elements of the good society breaks down when limited to descriptions of individuals. For example, consider the virtue of honesty. Would it be reasonable to expect that honest people working together would make honesty the norm in the workplace? It may be likely, but there could be circumstances that might restrict the honesty among certain individuals in the group. Total honesty and trust among workers might be hampered because of past relationships, work experiences, new leadership, or changes in power, authority, and organization. The virtue of honesty might not translate directly into honesty in the work group.

It should be no surprise that individual and group interests often conflict. Dewey proposed that each of us has our own perception of what we personally desire, and most of us can justify taking care of ourselves before considering the group's needs. For example, in Minnesota, mass transit is only minimally available. The metropolitan areas are nearing transportation gridlock due to inadequate highways and more cars on the roads. Yet many legislators are not willing to support mass transit, citing that their constituencies do not wish to give up driving their cars or pay the extra taxes required to build light rail or other transit. The debate is usually cast as the government encumbering the freedoms of individuals through higher taxes and asking people to ride buses and trains. It is precisely this type of public-private conflict that legislators must face if the situation is to be reformed.

In educational leadership, an attempt to reconcile the tensions between good groups and good individuals can be seen most clearly in the writings of Robert J. Starratt. A professor at Boston College, Starratt has been exploring the application of virtues to both schools and school leaders for at least the past 15 years.

His first major foray into this area was with his book *Building the Ethical School* (1994), in which he argued for the three virtues of care, justice, and critique in structuring a good school environment. Starratt proposed that a good school must seek to provide a strong sense of justice, it must ensure that there is a caring environment, and it must promote openness to critical inquiry and analysis. Reminding us of the continual struggle involved in building these kinds of schools, Starratt states that "virtue is not something we achieve and then continue to possess. We continue to be capable of doing evil. Virtue is always out in front of us to be achieved; it involves a perpetual doing" (pp. 135–136).

In *Ethical Leadership* (2004), Starratt describes the virtuous leader by presenting a "morality play" about a principal who is worried about the way his faculty provide instruction, especially for youngsters with special needs. In several reflective talks with a mentor, the principal is able to define his authentic beliefs and to identify what he needs to hold himself responsible for as a human being, administrator, and citizen. Three virtues—responsibility, authenticity, and presence—form the building blocks for this leader by interacting either in tension or by flowing the same direction. By focusing on these dynamics, Starratt shows us not only how complicated school leadership is, but that virtuous leadership is always under pressure.

While not specifically looking for congruence or dissonance between the school group attributes (care, justice, and critique) and the
leadership virtues (responsibility, authenticity, and presence), one can
ask the question, how might individual responsibility and authenticity
be mitigated by the need for just rules in a caring environment? Starratt
neither denies nor endorses such tensions, but he is very interested in
how the school leader might affect the goodness of a school.

CONFLICTING SOURCES OF ETHICAL TENSION

Ethical tension can be present in any given situation and can exist between any of the four sources. We have contrasted duties with desires
and have illustrated virtues of individuals clashing with groups. There
is also the tension that occurs when virtues of either individuals or
groups clash with our duties and desires. This is characterized as the
clash between who we are (virtue and good society ethics) and what we
believe or seek to accomplish (duties-based or desires-based ethics).

In figure 2.2, we contrast tensions that occur within each of four
quadrants. In the first quadrant, the tension between virtues and desires
is highlighted. This may occur when one's personal sense of excellence
and integrity (specific virtues) clashes with achieving a particular goal
within a limited time period (ends or outcomes). It may also occur
when personal values conflict with desires of the majority to which one
belongs. While we might acknowledge our affiliation with the group,
our personal values are at odds with what is desired by the group.

The second quadrant reflects the tension between conflicting desires
and outcomes among varied groups. As noted earlier, each of us is a
member of multiple social groupings, affiliations, and associations that
can be personal, professional, or cultural. The desires and expectations
of these varied groups may not be aligned, pulling us in different directions and creating stress as we decide what we desire. This tension
can be thought of as a clash of good society ethics with desires-based
ethics.

The tension present in the third quadrant is similar. The clash between different group affiliations may play out in what is deemed best
for the group (good society ethics) in contrast with the roles, responsi-

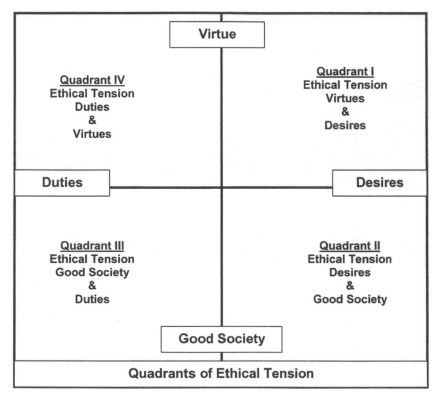

Figure 2.2.   Four Quadrants

bilities, and obligations of the members (duties-based ethics). For example, consider what happens when one's obligation to the family clashes with one's professional duties and responsibilities. Choosing between two equally important commitments can be stressful and challenging.

In the fourth quadrant, we see the tension between virtue ethics and duties, as for example when one faces a choice between telling the truth (the virtue of honesty) or remaining loyal to the group (fulfilling one's duty). It is also present when we personally disagree with a fundamental rule or law. Our obligation as a citizen is to follow the laws of the land, but if we are ethically opposed to the law, then tension between virtue and duty might exist. As illustrated, the sources of ethical tension deal with our perceived duties and desires as well as our definitions of the good person and the good society.

JUDGMENTS AND CONSEQUENCES

In the process of working through these ethical tensions, judgment is probably the most important skill that leaders can bring to a situation. We are expected to begin by gathering available information, reflecting upon the needs of the individuals involved, and considering probable outcomes. Having weighed the evidence and consequences, we are obliged to make the best possible decision given the circumstances.

What informs that judgment? Typically our judgments are framed by one or more of the ethical tensions described above. For example, we might have staunch beliefs about how we want something to turn out, or we might feel a strong sense of duty toward specific actions because of our responsibility as an educator. We might operate from virtues like truth, integrity, caring, or respectfulness, reflecting upon how they apply to the situation at hand. Hopefully we can remain open to others' views and not be obstinate to all compromise or excessively proud and stubborn in our own convictions. Perhaps we recognize the importance of collaboration with the community groups that we serve. But we also acknowledge that not all desires can be met and that subgroups might hold conflicting views. We might seek to understand the larger group's views and values in the particular situation. Such beliefs inform the judgments that we make.

We must also consider the consequences of our actions, specifically what we think is going to happen. The consequences may be internal or external, positive or negative. For example, suppose you decide for some reason to lie to your friend. As a result of this action, you feel guilty, a consequence that is internalized. An external consequence is the social approbation for an action. If you are publicly censured for your lying, this would be a negative external consequence, which might deter you from behaving in this manner again. Conversely, social approval or praise might encourage your actions, but should you always act in ways that garner praise and popularity? Ethical judgment requires weighing the possible positive and negative consequences of a given action.

When faced with a challenging situation that results in an ethical dilemma, it is expected that a leader will work through a process of reasoning and reflection in order to make a final judgment about what ac-

---

Problem/Situation
What has initiated the need for description?

Information gathering
What is necessary information and data?

Ethical systems
What are the sources of ethical tension? Duties-based versus desires-based, virtue ethics versus good society, or some other combination?

Judgment/Discernment
Can a judgment be made? Is there adequate information? If we do not have sufficient information, how might we reconsider and reflect upon the problem further by using the four ethical systems?

Consequences
What are the likely consequences? What are actual anticipated and unanticipated outcomes?

Resolution/Reflection
Is the problem resolved as a result of action taken? If not, how might we reconsider and revise our decision?

Figure 2.3.   Ethical Process

tion to take. In figure 2.3, we sketch how ethical decision making might occur from an initial problem through working toward some action. This process model shows how the four sources of ethical tension can be integrated in our deliberations when considering what action is to be taken.

As we embark on the process of ethical deliberation and decision making, it is helpful to remember the playwright Sophocles' advice in the Greek tragedy *Antigone*. The heroine Antigone has been condemned to death for her actions, and while she does not waver in her convictions, she demonstrates the kind of reflection that acknowledges the complexity of her situation. According to Badaracco (2006), Sophocles advises us that

> good deliberation is a messy process. It goes back and forth, often zigzagging among feelings, thoughts, facts, and analysis. It is discursive rather than linear. It doesn't forget the past. It also looks forward, with vivid imagination, to possible consequences. Good deliberation acknowledges clear duties as well as open-ended responsibilities. It weighs

and judges moral principles before applying them and again after applying them. And serious reflection does not seize a single grand principle—like duty to country or duty to the gods and family—and let it obliterate other considerations. (p. 175)

SUMMARY

In this chapter, we identified four different sources of ethical tension that occur when people deal with each other. The first source, duty-based ethics (also known as deontological ethics), relates to one's personal and professional duties that prescribe universal principles to be upheld by all (universalist). Second, desires-based ethics (teleological or ends-based ethics) focuses on what is deemed best for the majority (utilitarian). The third source of ethical tension emphasizes the individual's character and behavior (virtue ethics), which contrasts with the fourth source, the group or societal perspective on character and behavior (good society ethics).

Each source of ethical tension forms a system of assumptions and beliefs used in decision making. We have illustrated how these systems clash when people operate from different ethical perspectives. Conflicts can occur in any situation, can be internal as well as external, and can exist among all four of the sources. To work through these conflicts, leaders need to harness sound judgment and consider the consequences of each action. We briefly sketched a process model showing how the sources of ethical tension are embedded within deliberation. Discursive rather than linear, deliberation goes back and forth. It is no wonder that conflict resolution often looks difficult, messy, and irreconcilable.

CHAPTER 3

Religion and Religious Attitudes

Many of us find it challenging to discuss how religion, and particularly our own religious beliefs, relate to our professional lives. Some individuals view religious ideology to be deeply personal rather than professional, and thus not appropriate in discussing educational leadership. Others hold the view that public servants such as school leaders should discriminate between religious and secular matters, separating church and state. Still others do not see any division between acting ethically and professing a religious ideology in a public school setting. For them, doing what is right and good means demonstrating their religious beliefs in daily life. In teaching about ethics and school leadership, we have struggled to address these different perspectives and believe there is a need to do so in a book about leadership and ethics.

There are many ethical concerns that relate back to our religious orientation and ideology. In chapter 2, we discussed sources of ethical tension, namely how one's duties might clash with one's desires, with what are deemed virtues for one's self as well as for one's society, and so on. These sources of tension can be greatly influenced by the religious beliefs we hold about what makes a good person, what is the right thing to do, and what defines a moral-ethical society. As well, how we choose to decide about what action to take may be influenced by our particular religion. We might follow a creed like the Golden Rule: "Always treat others as you would like them to treat you" (Matthew 7:12). Perhaps we might seek divine inspiration through contemplative meditation practices. For these reasons, we seek to clarify the role of our religious values and beliefs in conducting ethical deliberation and decision making as educators working in public school settings.

We begin the chapter with a definition of religion and describe briefly how it has evolved as our society has become increasingly diversified and complex. Consideration is given to how our religious traditions inform the moral-ethical choices we make and determine what codes of conduct might contribute to our actions. By contrasting different religions, we highlight the variability among ideologies across and within religions. We also consider the religious freedom made available by our U.S. Constitution and practiced in American society. To move beyond the legal domain, we refer to Dewey's distinction between religion and religious attitude, which enables us to be more open to inquiry. Finally, we address the work expected of school administrators who need to honor religious freedom while accommodating diversity.

DEFINITION OF RELIGION

Derived from the Latin *ligo*, meaning "to tie or bind," the word *religion* originally meant being bound by vows to a particular way of life, as were *les religieux*, the monastics who assumed certain vows (Dewey, 1934, p. 23). Using the *Oxford Dictionary*, Dewey (1934) quotes the definition of religion to be "recognition on the part of man of some unseen higher power as having control of his destiny and as being entitled to obedience, reverence and worship" (p. 3).

In a more general sense, religion can connote being bound by obligations to whatever powers we believe govern our destiny and secure our way of life (Fasching & deChant, 2001, p. 11). Ancient peoples, for example, viewed nature with awe and revered the collective powers that provided life as well as destroyed it. Through myths and ritual, they honored the appropriate gods that brought a good harvest, fertility, prosperity, and victory in war. It was believed that failure to do so would bring famine, poverty, death, and destruction. The earliest religious stories were versions of how nature, either personified as gods, spirits, or magical forces, governed human destiny.

As tribal communities became less dependent upon nature and more complex in social organization, the view shifted from humans being arbitrarily at the whim of nature toward their being part of a divinely inspired cosmic plan. In such societies, customs or mores were regarded as sacred and unchangeable. What was done and how it was done were taken as the way they should be done. The word *morality* was derived from the Latin root (*mos, mores*) that meant "customs" of the people. "Morality is an inherent dimension of the sacred order of society. In large part, what gives a society social stability is the sense that its way of life is sacred and unchangeable" (Fasching & deChant, 2001, p. 14).

Sociologist Emile Durkheim viewed religion as the "human response to the overwhelming (and therefore sacred) power of society upon which we depend for our existence," and the purpose of religious myths was "to sacralize society so that its customs can be considered sacred and bring social stability to human life" (Fasching & deChant, 2001, pp. 14–15). Tribal peoples honored their ancestors, revered totems, and recounted myths to bring about that social stability. In more complex societies, we find religion providing meaning for life and providing the stability needed to weather the inevitable uncertainties of contemporary living.

In a similar vein, Max Weber concurred that religion functioned to sanction the "routine order" of society, but he also proposed that it could at times bring about dramatic social change. For example, the Roman Catholic Church served to uphold the social order during the Middle Ages but was called into question by Martin Luther, who led the Protestant Reformation and challenged the church's proprietary establishment. A new religious order and authority were replacing what had been held to be sacred.

While religious practices have served to order and give meaning to our lives, secular ideologies such as scientific reasoning and technology have challenged them. For instance, geological discoveries have displaced creation myths, and the biological sciences, particularly research in genetics, have revolutionized current thinking about mind-body connections. Fasching and deChant (2001) briefly describe how science emerged, beginning as early as the 17th century, to replace religion.

In Europe in the seventeenth, eighteenth, and nineteenth centuries, science emerged and replaced the religious stories of origin and destiny of the world with secular, rationalistic, non-religious stories. In the nineteenth and twentieth centuries this way of viewing the world was spread to virtually all cultures around the globe through colonialism—the European political and economic domination of the world's cultures. At the beginning of the nineteenth century, it seemed as if the great missionary movements of Christianity, which accompanied colonialism around the globe, would overcome all other religions. By the end of the century, it was beginning to look as if science was replacing all religions and that religion itself would soon disappear. In this world, human beings were no longer supposed to be guided in their public life by their ancient sacred stories but by scientific and technical reason. (p. 49)

But that was not to be the case. The utopian belief that science and technology would lead to progress was severely compromised given the events of World War II, culminating in the mass destruction of lives at Auschwitz and Hiroshima. According to Fasching and deChant (2001), "Technical experts were not supposed to raise ethical questions about mass death: they were supposed to follow orders with unquestioning obedience" (p. 55). If through such bureaucratic rationalization we could condone acts of mass murder, then we needed moral-ethical principles to direct our lives. For that, as a people, we again turned back to religious traditions, institutions, and ideology, but with much greater variability and diversity, as evident in our global society.

RELIGIOUS TRADITIONS

As in the past, religious traditions promote values that specify the meaning of life. In Christianity, for example, redemption is found in the Kingdom of God through his son, Jesus Christ. A meaningful life can be achieved by following Jesus's teachings and living a similar life. For Buddhists, the inevitable suffering (*dukkha*) of human life can be ended and enlightenment (*nirvana*) attained, as demonstrated by the Buddha himself. In the Hindu-ethical tradition that originated around 1500 BCE, meaning is to be found in who you are as well as in what stage of life you have reached in a defined caste. By following the natural order, a Hindu practitioner can generate positive effects (karma) and reap benefits in the next life (Bilimoria, 1991, p. 47).

Religious traditions, institutions, and ideology also prescribe how we should live. For example, Judaism teaches that the right way is to observe the Torah, which are revelations of the will of God. In some 613 commandments, the Torah specifies roles and relationships (e.g., parent to child, husband to wife); laws; diet; and other rules for living. Among the best known are the Ten Commandments and the Levitical Code. According to Kellner (1991), one of the basic contributions of Judaism to the Western religious tradition is "that one worships God through decent, humane, and moral relations with one's fellows" (p. 84). Derived from the same roots as Judaism and Christianity, Islam is a theistic religion based on the belief that there is one God (Allah), and it includes prophets like Abraham, Moses, and Jesus. The Prophet Muhammad, the founder of Islam, taught that obedience to God required submission, which brought about unity, brotherhood, righteousness, and peace. A devout follower (a Muslim) was expected to observe the Five Pillars of Islam, each a part of the right action that leads to becoming a good person.

By contrast, Buddhism is a religion that is nontheistic and does not have a belief in God; nevertheless, it offers a set of guidelines for one's spiritual development. Buddhist teachings are based on the Four Noble Truths, which define human suffering, its cause, its cessation, and the means to its end (Armstrong, 2001). The way to end suffering is through the Eightfold Path, a code of conduct about right beliefs, ideals, words, deeds, livelihoods, efforts, thinking, and meditation. Through diligent commitment, a Buddhist practitioner can overcome the suffering caused by greed, hatred, and illusion while developing a way of life leading toward peace, joy, and insight.

Variation of a given religion might occur among its branches or sects, where some followers take a more conservative interpretation of the religion than others do. For example, within the Jewish faith today, the Orthodox, Conservative, and Reform sects all accept the moral and ethical teachings of Judaism but differ in their observance of the ceremonial and ritual laws. Orthodox believers keep strictly to the traditional ceremonial regulations as found in the Torah, the compilation of the teachings (Talmud), and the later books by religious leaders. Conservative Jews, while recognizing the authority of Jewish ritual law, have chosen to adopt a number of modifications in practice. Those who are Reform Jews generally place less emphasis on the rituals and tend to use the teachings as general guiding principles, not as precepts. They consider the spirit of the faith even more important than the letter of the law.

Derivations of Christian morality vary not only from one denomination to another but can rely upon different sources of authority (Thompson, 2003). At the time of the Protestant Reformation, for instance, Luther challenged the authority of the Roman Catholic Church on the basis of the authority of the scriptures. Since that time, reason and conscience have played an important role in reexamining and exploring a Protestant's moral action. Islamic sects can also vary by sources of authority. In the Middle East, the two largest sects of Muslims formed after the Prophet Muhammad died and followers split among the successors. Those who followed Abu Bakr and Omar became Sunni, while the followers of the Prophet Muhammad's cousin Ali became Shiites. Notably, the Shiites uphold a Muslim tradition tied to the spiritual authority vested in the imam, a designated spiritual teacher or his representatives, acknowledged to be the custodian of its Holy book (the Koran) and the Prophet Muhammad's teachings (Nanji, 1991). Though less numerous than the Sunni, the Shiites have challenged them for religious and political leadership in parts of Saudi Arabia, Iran, Iraq, North Africa, and Pakistan.

The religious values of one specific tradition may apply to society in general, not only to the members of that religious persuasion. For example, many ethical arguments in our American society espouse Christian values (e.g., belief in God; salvation through God's son, Jesus Christ; love of one's enemies). Indeed, Christianity has had a prominent role in our country's history and culture, with societal practices viewed to be habitual and "natural." Evidence can be found in our coinage (e.g., "In God we trust"), our ceremonies (e.g., saying the pledge of allegiance), and our rituals (e.g., taking an oath of office using a Bible). But not all American citizens are of the Christian faith, and in a democratic society where freedom of religion is practiced, they should not have to be.

A religious tradition might be so much a part of a sociocultural fabric that it may be difficult to determine what its religious values and beliefs are as contrasted with the moral-ethical values of that society. Dating back to 1500 BCE, Hinduism exemplifies not one specific religion but can refer to various religious traditions of the South Asian subcontinent, all serving to define the morally good life and specify right conduct. Bilimoria (1991) states that Indian ethics might be described as "the 'soul' of the complex spiritual and moral aspirations of the people, co-mingled with social and political structures forged over a vast period of time" (p. 43). As such, it reflects an "incredibly diversified collection of social, cultural, religious and philosophical systems" that has changed over time.

Branches or sects within a religious tradition can evolve across different societies as well as change over time. For example, while Buddhism originated in India, it took root in many Asian countries, creating varied sects like Chan Buddhism, which arose in China and later became Zen practice in Japan. The cultures of India, China, and Japan contributed much to the development and evolution of Zen Buddhism in those respective countries. Thompson (2003) states that "it is not simply a matter of understanding the religious and cultural norms of each group, but of sorting out to which group a person is giving his or her loyalty at any one time. Such diversity also affects religions that cross cultures" (p. 164).

Adding to this complexity, each religious tradition may present seemingly contradictory moral and ethical directions. On the one hand, individuals are directed to follow religious precepts and be good in order to be justly rewarded. Thus, they should follow prudent reasoning and act in their own self-interest to be duly rewarded rather than punished. On the other hand, individuals are to uphold the ethical ideal of selflessness in caring for the well-being of others. Philosophers call this an appeal to "moral reason" to do what benefits others before oneself.

Which directive is correct? In *Religion and Moral Reason* (1988), philosopher Ronald Green proposes that there are stages of spiritual growth and development. The seemingly contradictory advice needs to be understood as different directions for individuals at varied stages; "stories of punishment and reward are meant for beginners in the moral and spiritual life, while the stories of selfless love and compassion are meant for those more advanced" (Fasching & deChant, 2001, p. 31). Ultimately, it is hoped that one's religious tradition provides a comprehensive set of stories, rituals, and spiritual practices to support one's spiritual evolution.

In sum, we have attempted to present examples of how different religious traditions provide meaning and spiritual direction for our lives. This may be directed toward a teleological end that defines meaning and purpose in life. Or it may be in the form of codes of conduct or precepts to follow as deontological constraints on our actions. Depending on the religious tradition, these codes may vary according to different interpretations of the law, different branches or sects, or different governing authorities. Religious institutions and ideologies have evolved over time and across distance, from the country of origin to the country of adoption. As we evolve in our thinking and reflection, so too does our understanding of our religious ideology and the traditions directing our moral conduct and ethical action.

RELIGIOUS FREEDOM

The first article of our U.S. Bill of Rights states that "Congress shall make no law respecting an establishment of religion, or prohibiting the free exercise thereof," which enables individuals to worship as they see fit. Furthermore, they are entitled to not worship at all if that is their belief. By directive of our U.S. Constitution, the national government must permit full religious freedom to its citizens. In the years since America was founded, state governments have made similar provisions to protect religious freedom.

However, in practice our religious tolerance as a society has been limited. Until the late 1960s, tolerance in the public school setting applied only to different kinds of Protestant religious expressions. Catholic practitioners historically found that public schools were sufficiently unfriendly to their tradition and chose to start a separate school system altogether (Strike, Haller, & Soltis, 1998). Non-Christian religious followers have been particularly marginalized for being nontheistic (e.g., Buddhist or Confucian beliefs), for observing different practices (e.g., the Muslim tradition of praying five times a day), and for commemorating holy days other than Christian ones (e.g., the Jewish Sabbath beginning at sundown on Fridays).

Legally, the U.S. Supreme Court has since ruled that conducting prayer or Bible readings in public school forums is in violation of the First Article of the Bill of Rights. Also illegal are acts such as endorsing a particular religion over another, promoting religion against being nonreligious, and proselytizing in public school settings. What schools can legally do is provide transportation, books, and other materials, as well as support services, to religious schools. They may provide accommodations for students who have religious conflicts with aspects of the curriculum or for scheduling around religious observances. If schools permit nonreligious groups to use their facilities, then they must do the same for religious groups (Shapiro & Stefkovich, 2005).

DISTINGUISHING RELIGION FROM RELIGIOUS ATTITUDE

Beyond the legal domain, it is appropriate to consider how we make moral-ethical decisions from our religious traditions. For considering this, Dewey (1934) offers a helpful distinction between religion and the "religious." While the noun *religion* "always signifies a special body of beliefs and practices having some kind of institutional organization, loose or tight" (p. 9), the adjective *religious* denotes "attitudes that may be taken toward every object and every proposed end or ideal" (p. 10). Dewey's distinction indicates that a "religious" attitude is much more general and can apply to that which is outside of organized or formal religion.

To illustrate the religious aspect of experience, Dewey relates the story of a writer who, on the verge of a nervous breakdown, resolves to set aside time daily to relate his life to God. This reorientation brings him a sense of security and peace. While there is a particular religion emphasized in this story in terms of the writer relating to a personal God, Dewey suggests that persons of other religions (e.g., Taoists, Buddhists, Muslims, and even atheists like the philosopher Spinoza) might have experienced similar kinds of transformations.

> The way in which the experience operated, its function, determines its religious value. If the reorientation actually occurs, it, and the sense of the security and stability accompanying it, are forces on their own account. It takes place in different persons in a multitude of ways. (Dewey, 1934, p. 14)

While religions claim to have this effect of reorientation and change of will, Dewey suggests that "whenever this change takes place there is a definitely religious attitude. . . . When it occurs, from whatever cause and by whatever means, there is a religious outlook and function" (p. 17). Unlike religion itself, this kind of attitude is not bounded or tied to a particular way of life or specific institution; rather, it can be much broader and can even be expressed through art, science, or good citizenship. For Dewey, this religious attitude promotes understanding and knowledge based upon continuous and rigorous inquiry. Such an attitude would be different from one that is limited in scope and dependent upon dogma or a specific interpretation of doctrine.

Iranian writer Azar Nafisi (2005) exemplifies this distinction between religion and religious attitude as she recalls a scene from Mark Twain's *Huckleberry Finn*. In this scene, the young Huck Finn contemplates what to do about his friend Jim, a runaway slave:

> Huck asks himself whether he should give Jim up or not. Huck was told in Sunday School that people who let slaves go free go to "everlasting fire." But then, Huck says he imagines he and Jim in "the day and nighttime, sometimes moonlight, sometimes storms, and we a-floating along, talking and singing and laughing." Huck remembers Jim and their friendship and warmth. He imagines Jim not as a slave but as a human being and he decides that, "alright then, I'll go to hell."

Nafisi goes on to explain how this story relates to her own experiences in Tehran.

> What Huck rejects is not religion but an attitude of self-righteousness and inflexibility. I remember this particular scene out of *Huck Finn* so vividly today, because I associate it with a difficult time in my own life. In the early 1980s when I taught at the University of Tehran, I, like many others, was expelled. I was very surprised to discover that my staunchest allies were two students who were very active at the University's powerful Muslim Students' Association. These young men and I had engaged in very passionate and heated arguments. I had fiercely opposed their ideological stances. But that didn't stop them from defending me. When I ran into one of them after my expulsion, I thanked him for his support. "We are not as rigid as you imagine us to be, Professor Nafisi," he responded. "Remember your own lectures on Huck Finn? Let's just say, he is not the only one who can risk going to hell!"

The religious attitude that Dewey distinguished is evident in Huckleberry Finn's rejection of an attitude of self-righteousness, as noted by Professor Nafisi. But more powerfully, it is learned and practiced by her Iranian students as they defended her right to teach. As Dewey states, it is an attitude that promotes understanding through knowledge.

THE SACRED AND THE HOLY

Fasching and deChant (2001) offer another way to consider this kind of transcendent religious attitude. The distinction between religion and the religious is evident in what is held to be *sacred* in contrast with what is considered *holy*. *Sacred* refers to an ordering of society in terms of morality, that is, knowing what ought to be done and is obligatory. In early tribal societies, this meant honoring the gods or spirits to ensure that goodness would prevail. In contemporary times, the notion of sacred reflects what we hold important and cherish about our society. Accordingly, "even modern societies that do not explicitly appeal to established religious stories tend to exhibit a sacred morality" (p. 14). For example, if the American flag is burned or a cross is desecrated, then we might find those acts offensive. While flag burning is clearly a political act and the other is more obviously tied to the Christian religion, both are examples of objects held to be sacred and honored in our country. In a similar way, the Muslim world was recently outraged by cartoons that depicted their Prophet Mohammed and implicated him as a terrorist. Publishing these cartoons represents an act that was sacrilegious and disrespectful to Muslims worldwide.

Contrasting with the sacred, the experience of the holy encourages us to consider wholeness rather than right versus wrong. According to Fasching and deChant (2001), "The task of an ethic of holy is not to eliminate the morality of society, but to transform it by breaking down the divisions between the sacred and the profane through narratives of hospitality to the stranger, which affirm the human dignity of precisely those who do not share one's identity and one's stories" (p. 18). This is essentially the religious attitude that Dewey was distinguishing, one that draws from the diversity and richness of having a pluralistic society. It enables questioning and encourages us to deconstruct what we hold to be sacred. This kind of critique advances societal thinking and promotes human dignity. "While a sacred society is founded on a shared set of answers that belong to the finite world of 'the way things are,' a holy community is founded on experiences of openness to the infinite . . . seeing and acting on new possibilities" (p. 19).

As the sacred and the holy propose different ways to think about our traditions and beliefs, we advocate not choosing one over the other. Rather, we invite the reader to consider what is sacred and needing to be preserved in our society. What do we hold to be important, and why? Are these values and beliefs shared, and by whom? As well, consider what is deemed holy, that which brings us together as a community. What are the ways to think about who we are as a people that can unite rather than divide us? What traditions and beliefs emphasize our collective unity rather than our deep divisions? Both notions of the sacred and the holy can be useful in thinking through what we believe and value individually and collectively.

ADMINISTRATIVE WORK

In our work as school administrators, regardless of our religious traditions and beliefs, we must honor the freedoms permitted by our democratic society. Legally, we are obligated to abide by the U.S. Constitution as interpreted by the Supreme Court. Religious beliefs are a private matter, and as such, we respect the free choice of individuals to profess their faith in whatever way they choose. Different from times past when one was born into a particular faith because of one's family background (e.g., when to be Irish meant to be Catholic), individuals today are much freer to decide their religious values, beliefs, and practices based on their own volition. They may be raised in one faith tradition, convert to another as adults, and partner with someone of yet another religious orientation. There are more choices to believe and practice freely in our American society. Perhaps because of this freedom to choose, individuals hold more steadfastly to their convictions. According to Strike et al. (1998),

> Religious convictions are often central to people's conception of who they are and what their fundamental duties and obligations are. To treat

religious convictions as objects of potential public interest is to open a path for doing great violence to individuals. We treat religious belief and practice as largely a private matter not so much because these things have no public consequences, but because they have such profound personal consequences. (p. 35)

We also recognize that we are members of a civil society that accommodates diversity and differences. There is no singular religious institution fundamental to our social order and organization; rather, there are varied social institutions formed for educational, political, economic, philanthropic, and scientific purposes that occur independently of any religion. All of these social institutions influence how we associate and interact with one another. This was noted in chapter 2 as we spoke of ethical tensions created by our affiliations and the responsibilities of membership in them.

Our work as educational leaders positions us as a fulcrum, honoring individuals' values and beliefs while teaching tolerance and accommodating diversity. Schools can be places where youngsters learn about different histories, cultures, religious beliefs, and values. They can also be places for discussion and debate where students learn to respect as well as critique alternative perspectives. We believe that students should have the opportunity to think for themselves about what is just and right, good and caring. They need to develop their capacity to reflect upon their views, defend their positions, and even change their minds. By the same token, schools need to respect a student's right to disagree, as Strike et al. (1998) suggest in the following example. Suppose a student's religion teaches that homosexuality is a sin. "Schools might explain . . . that homosexuals are entitled to equal rights regardless of whether homosexuality is a sin. But schools need not insist that these students view homosexuality as merely an alternative lifestyle" (p. 127).

We propose that to do this administrative work in public schools involves an ethic of democratic leadership. It requires human intelligence, which Dewey (1934) calls "ardor in behalf of light shining into the murky places of social existence, and as zeal for its refreshing and purifying effect" (p. 79). Intelligence directed toward justice and security, he says, is evident in human nature. "Human beings have impulses toward affection, compassion and justice, equality and freedom. It remains to weld all these things together" (p. 81).

SUMMARY

In this chapter, we explored how our religious views might influence the antecedent beliefs that form our decisions. Beginning with a definition of religion and how it has evolved as societies have diversified, we considered how our religious traditions inform our moral-ethical choices. These traditions provide direction for what we deem to be a good person, what is right action, and what defines a moral-ethical society. We also considered religious freedom as a guaranteed right of American citizenship that should be protected within our schools. Beyond this legal dimension, Dewey's notion of religious attitude enables us to be more open to inquiry. As well, the distinction between the sacred and the holy can be used to think through what we value and believe. We reflected upon the work expected of administrators who need to honor religious freedom while accommodating multiple perspectives.

CHAPTER 4

Feminist Ethics and Beyond

In our increasingly global society, we recognize that differing socio-cultural groups have contrasting philosophies about what makes for right action and desirable outcomes. In the previous chapters, we identified various sources of ethical tension and diverse religious traditions that create conflicts as individuals and groups live together. Nowhere is such conflict more evident than in our public schools. Students bring their unique sociocultural backgrounds—backgrounds as diverse as a first-generation Pacific Islander and a Minnesota urbanite, an African American Methodist and an Indian American Sikh, or a deaf soccer player and a gifted musician—into our public schools and under our sphere of influence. These students do not check their diversity at the school door, nor do they leave behind their family backgrounds and ethnic origins. Neither do they bring only part of who they are, leaving their special needs and abilities behind. As one educator reminded us, "The youngsters who come to our schools bring the very best of themselves."

As school leaders, our work is twofold. First, we are charged with serving all of our students fairly, equitably, and respectfully. That involves recognizing the individual differences and sociocultural backgrounds that they bring. It is about being open to others who might be different from us and providing educational options for the children in our care. A second aim of our work as educational leaders is to honor the shared values and beliefs that unify us as a democratic society. It means preparing our students to become successful and productive citizens, valued for their contributions and capable of working together.

We propose that these two aims are highly related to becoming effective, democratic leaders who make ethical judgments in diverse settings.

To further address the tasks of school leadership outlined above, we offer a theoretical lens—feminism—that has us look particularly at the differences that women bring to making ethical choices. Our rationale for presenting this perspective is to suggest how a critical theory can frame ethical issues and provide alternative yet equally valid ways to resolve and reconcile conflicts. It is especially useful because it offers a means for questioning and critiquing what we take for granted and encourages the direction of actions toward ethical deliberation. We begin with a definition of feminism and its three tenets. By focusing on areas in which feminism has been applied, we suggest ways to think about ethical decision making, and we consider school administrative work from a feminist perspective. Like all theories, feminism has its limitations, and these are also discussed. We conclude by proposing a move beyond the limitations of the theory with a more comprehensive version of feminism as it can be applied to ethical leadership.

DEFINITION OF FEMINISM

The term *feminism*, according to Houston (1996), refers broadly to the feminist theory and social movement that advocate for creating a society where women can live full, self-determined lives. Historian Joan Kelly characterizes feminism as having three tenets:

> (1) a deliberate and conscious opposition to male defamation and mistreatment of women; (2) a belief that the sexes are culturally and not just biologically formed, that women are a social group shaped by male notions of their sex; and (3) a desire for a conception of humanity that recognizes women as fully human. (Kelly as referenced in Houston, 1996, p. 215)

The first tenet of feminism echoes the struggle for women's rights. The "first wave" in the struggle was the women's suffrage movement, which in the United States can be traced back to Elizabeth Cady Stanton's declaration of women's rights at the Seneca Falls Convention in

1848. It would be another 72 years before American women actually did attain voting rights in 1920. Contrastingly, these full rights of citizenship were accorded to white men in the 18th century during the American Revolution. The "second wave" in the struggle occurred in the 1960s, with attention drawn to the civil rights of women, minorities, and marginalized peoples. Major sociopolitical institutions like the government, economy, and educational systems were criticized, as were social conventions such as marriage, family, and sexuality.

This evolution of the feminist movement from the 1960s into the 1980s relates to the second tenet, a critique that the "sexes are culturally, and not just biologically formed" (Houston, 1996, p. 215). The concept of "gender" emerged as distinct from biological sexuality. That is, to be a woman was *not* the same as to be female; *woman* refers to one's social, cultural, and political positioning within a given society within a specific time period, whereas *female* simply distinguishes one from being male. As feminism evolved, formulating the concept of gender has revealed new aspects of male dominance in areas never before acknowledged. Also, social factors such as one's class, race, ethnicity, sexual orientation, and age were seen as determinants of how one's gender was regarded. This acknowledgment pushed feminists to consider the multiple ways that sociocultural variables have confounded women's experiences and maintained structures of domination.

The third tenet of feminism advocates for women being fully recognized as fellow human beings. This tenet was expressed by the National Organization for Women (NOW) in its seeking "full equality for women in a truly equal partnership with men." As women were viewed as subordinates to men in all social spheres, the organization sought to make change in the workplace, home, and civic circles. But later, with greater political advocacy, NOW professed bolder goals of "women's liberation" and campaigned for legal and financial equality, equal work opportunity, and other emancipatory demands (Delmar, 2001). Extending beyond American borders, the organization promoted issues of human rights and dignity to end the domination of women worldwide.

Significant strides in the feminist movement have been made in our country. In the political arena, these include legislating for affirmative action, passing the Equal Rights Amendment in Congress, and electing more women politicians. In economics, strides have been made in closing the wage gap between men and women and in providing more professional avenues of employment for women. Certain social mores such as recognizing lesbian and gay relationships have been liberalized. Focusing on violence against women, advocates have raised awareness of domestic violence and of the prevalence of sexual harassment of girls. Others have worked in health and human services to provide essential health care for women, shelters for battered women and families, and 24-hour rape crisis centers. Some advocates have lobbied for self-determination through affirming abortion rights for women and teens. Still others have targeted pornography and violence resulting from the denigration of women in the media.

Beyond American borders, feminists have linked with those in Third World as well as developed nations to promote international resolutions for human dignity. Activists have worked to establish fair wages and to ensure educational opportunities for women. As in the United States, they have opposed violence, rape, sexual slave trades, and the general exploitation of women.

FEMINISM APPLIED

In focusing on gender inequities, feminist scholarship in education has attempted to uncover and dislodge white-male-dominated frameworks within institutions, work life, and social structures. Marshall (1997) suggests that feminist and critical theories offer useful lenses for looking at schools and asking the following kinds of questions: How is this policy or political action affected by gender roles? Why do social class, race-ethnicity, and gender inequities persist in this school or school system? To what extent does a certain high school promote curriculum and instructional practices that reinforce stereotypes of masculinity and femininity? What shapes the recruitment and retention of educational administrators that preferences white males? Why might leadership be oriented primarily toward bureaucracy and organizational efficiency at the expense of relationships and caregiving?

> There is room for decades of policy research which asks first, how does this policy or structure exclude certain publics (subordinate nationalities, religions, women, the urban poor, the working class, homosexuals), then

asks, what political arrangements support policies and structures that devalue alternative perspectives, that reinforce gender, ethnic/race and class inequities, and asks, who benefits from these arrangement, and finally, what are possible ways to restructure power dynamics and political arrangements to address issues of social justice. (Marshall, 1997, p. 2)

Such scholarship can be categorized into three complementary yet distinctive areas of study as depicted in table 4.1. The first area involves work within the system. The assumption is that equity will be achieved when barriers to gender are eliminated and when women attain positions of power and influence within the existing system. Examples of this area are policies such as affirmative action, the Equal Rights Amendment, and Title IX. A limitation of this perspective is that those who currently hold power and privilege have essentially created the sexism and racism that is denigrating others. Moreover, it might be naive to expect that those who hold power would willingly change and yield power to those without power and marginalized.

A second area of study reflects the view that women's ways of knowing and taking action are fundamentally different from those of men. In her groundbreaking book *In a Different Voice*, psychologist Carol Gilligan (1982) provides empirical evidence to support a feminist revision of moral development. Human development theory had been founded on the masculine myth of the hero's journey in which male experiences set the standard. Gilligan's mentor Lawrence Kohlberg conducted a longitudinal study of 84 men from childhood to adulthood. On the basis of the study, he proposed a model of six developmental stages of moral judgment where individuals were thought to evolve from preconventional to mature responses to ethical problems. On Kohlberg's scale, women were usually judged to be less ethically mature than men because of their responses.

However, in studying 11-year-old boys and girls, Gilligan found that the girls saw the ethical problem differently than the boys did. For the girls, the challenge was to sustain relationships, not necessarily to ensure justice, as was the case for the boys. Gilligan concluded that women were not less morally developed; rather, they chose to employ care for and sensitivity to the needs of others when making ethical decisions. This research points toward the need to question fundamental assumptions of similarity and difference between the genders. Unlike

Table 4.1. Feminist Areas of Study

Area of Study	Focus	Assumptions	Examples	Limitations
Equity	More equitable treatment and opportunities within established systems.	When barriers based upon gender are broken down, then equity will be achieved.	Affirmative action, equal rights, Title IX nondiscrimination policies.	Assumes that those who hold power and are responsible for current systems will change.
Women's ways of knowing	Women's experience of the world is different from men's and should be honored.	By honoring women's ways of knowing, women become full partners in any endeavor.	Gilligan's development of an ethic of care as different from but as viable as an ethic of justice.	Can be interpreted as essentialist, universal, and enduring.
Power	Deconstruction of power relationships, inequitable structures, rules, patterns, and language.	For true equity to be achieved, systems must be redesigned. Rules and patterns must be established to balance power.	Ferguson's study of how bureaucracies control and stifle women.	Power relationships are often embedded in culture and norms, and thus are difficult to detect.

men, women do not necessarily follow similar patterns, nor should they be deemed less or inferior but merely different.

Power is the third area of study in which feminism identifies aspects of the purposes and processes within an organization or system that create and maintain gender inequities. For example, Ferguson (1984) identifies ways in which structures, rules, language, and patterns of domination in bureaucracies serve to control women, benefiting from their work while stifling their alternative ways of talking, valuing, and living their lives. Boldly, she advocates for a nonbureaucratic approach to organizations, "conceiving the individual and the collective that reflects the care taking and nurturant experiences embedded in women's role" (Ferguson, 1984, p. x).

As feminist scholars pursue this research, they might consider the informal as well as the formal mechanisms of sexism, an organization's historical precedence for male domination, and value-laden assumptions that have silenced or stifled minorities. Unfortunately, because power relations within organizations and systems can be embedded and nested, decoupling power and gender in order to decipher inequities may be challenging.

ADMINISTRATIVE WORK FROM A FEMINIST PERSPECTIVE

In the early development of school administration, John Franklin Brown (1909) published what became a classic text for high school principals entitled *The American High School*. Regarding the importance of gender among the qualifications for principalship, he wrote,

> Generally speaking, men make better principals than women, especially in large schools. They are stronger physically; they possess more executive ability; they are more likely to command the confidence of male citizens; they are more judicial in mind; they are more sure to seize upon the essential merits of a question; they are less likely to look at things from a personal point of view; they are likely to be better supported by subordinates; and simply because they are men, they are more likely to command fully the respect and confidence of boys. (pp. 241–242)

Nearly a hundred years later, the perception remains that men make better principals than women, especially at the secondary school level, for the same reasons given by Brown in the early 20th century. Men are viewed as physically stronger, appear to be more rational and objective, and have the ability to "rally the troops" toward action, especially in handling the rowdy and belligerent.

In considering a feminist perspective, we challenge such a perception and question whether it is based exclusively upon men's experiences. As Ferguson (1984); Gilligan (1982); and Belenky, Clinchy, Goldberger, and Tarule (1986) have done, we consider whether there might be perceived differences between women and men because of differing social upbringings and culture. For example, do men and women make decisions differently? Should women's decision making be measured against men's? Are women's ways of knowing and deciding equally worthy of consideration? If so, then why have we historically stifled or silenced their voices? How might we be more inclusive of their experiences?

As more women hold professional positions or political office, there is more support for appointing woman administrators to manage and lead schools and school districts. In terms of experience, women continue to dominate the field of teaching and thus bring more years of classroom experience to the task of being instructional leaders in schools. They also have entered graduate education programs in greater numbers to become better teachers or to seek administrative certification and advanced degrees. There are more women serving as elementary school principals than ever before. In sum, women bring teaching experience, graduate education, and administrative preparation to demonstrate their competence for holding administrative positions at the secondary and system levels.

But it is not sufficient to increase the numbers of women in administrative positions and eliminate the barriers that prevent women from accessing positions of power and influence. A feminist perspective on administrative work demands that equal consideration be given to values traditionally deemed "feminine," such as caregiving, nurturance, relationship development, and community building. Rather than dismissing these values as subjective and personalized, a feminist perspective honors the importance of caregiving within educational settings, challenging all who serve as administrators to draw upon their emotions as well as intellect to understand student needs (Noddings, 1992).

In *The Least of These*, a fictional account of an urban elementary school principal, Mary Van Cleave (1994) writes about placing priority on the needs of children. Rather than addressing declining test scores by remediation or by fine-tuning the curriculum, she believes that the first job of teachers should be the children. She writes of this from the perspective of the principal, Marilyn Wallace:

> We have some other things to do first. We need to make the children as secure as we can. We need to see who they are—what they like and don't like, what their strengths are. Let's give them a school where they can get their hands on things, get involved in projects that answer the questions they have about their world. Let's let them talk to us and to each other. I don't care about the test scores. I *really* don't care. What matters is that the children have a school where they feel safe and secure and loved, where they feel as if they have something to contribute, where they feel their own worth. If we can work together to create that kind of environment, they'll learn everything we want them to learn—and more. (Van Cleave, 1994, p. 15)

An administrator who holds a feminist perspective will raise issues about how a school privileges some and oppresses others. Not only is gender discrimination considered, but class, race-ethnicity, age, sexual orientation, and other means of marginalizing youngsters are uncovered. Are there ways in which school practices categorize, stereotype, and thereby exclude certain individuals or groups from equal access, open enrollment, and free participation? How are teachers and staff supported in understanding the different sociocultural groups within the school? Or is there a mentality about assimilating and socializing all youngsters in the same way throughout the American public education system? What are the success rates and achievements among different groups of students? Do certain groups require assistance or remediation? If so, is there a "blame-the-victim" approach to providing that assistance? To what extent does the school encourage alternative instructional practices that might be culturally sensitive? School administrators can be key in promoting equal opportunity and equitable treatment that enable students to succeed despite the challenges of poverty, second-language learning, and special needs.

LIMITATIONS OF A FEMINIST PERSPECTIVE

Because feminism evolved from acknowledging women's perspectives, a fundamental limitation is that the perspective might be viewed strictly as "women's work" and be exclusively reserved for only women to undertake. Among the sharpest critics of feminism have been those who hold traditional views of the role of women as homemakers and primary caregivers in the private domain. They argue for retaining this exclusivity. By contrast, feminists advocate that women's worlds should not to be limited or bounded within the private domain. Women's contributions in social, economic, and political arenas attest to doing so.

A second limitation is that feminism tends to view women collectively, making their perspective essentialized. Belenky et al. (1986) proposed that women's ways of acquiring and organizing knowledge were fundamentally different from men's. Yet as was noted earlier, not all women's experiences and ways of knowing are necessarily similar. Specifically, women of color and on the margins such as lesbians, Jewish women, Native American women, and older women have felt that their lived experiences as women and minorities are not reflected in the feminist discourse. While white women might be victims of one system of domination because of their gender, they have remained agents of domination because of their "whiteness." This criticism has demanded that feminists reconsider whose perspectives are being reflected and what other social factors might confound women's experiences.

A counterargument can be drawn from postmodern thinkers like Richard Rorty who suggests that we recognize and celebrate the multiplicity of viewpoints. "Constructing gender is a process, not an answer. In using a postmodernist approach, we open the possibility of theorizing gender in heretofore unimagined ways. Postmodernism allows us to see that as observers of gender we are also its creators" (Hare-Mustin & Marecek, 2001, p. 102). A feminist perspective can become an evolving viewpoint that honors difference—female-male, young-old, white-nonwhite, gay-straight—and that attempts to be inclusive rather than exclusive in its orientation. Christian eco-feminist Rosemary Ruether (1992) proposes that "what unites us in a common struggle and social vision is far more important than the differences that distinguish us" (p. xix).

A third limitation of feminism arises from trying to be all things to everyone, accommodating the depth and breadth of women's experiences. A challenge has been to define a theoretical stance that places women at the center and yet includes the varied life experiences of marginalized women and minorities. While most advocates direct their efforts against gender oppression, some voice criticism about a feminism that generalizes from white, middle-class women's experiences. "The problem of how to create feminist theory that reflects the reality of women and avoids a monolithic view of women remains unresolved. The task is both to maintain the category *women* and at the same time embrace the differences within this category" (Houston, 1996, p. 218).

As with many applications of theory, there is a divide between feminist theory and how it is practiced, and proponents push for more pragmatic action to replace academic theorizing. "Feminist activists point out that re-describing and creating new meaning in theory is not enough to stop battering, promote reproductive freedom, or end child abuse" (Houston, 1996, p. 218). For some, the ultimate end of feminism is the total eradication of domination and oppression. According to bell hooks (1984),

> Feminism is a commitment to eradicating the ideology of domination that permeates Western culture on various levels—sex, race, class to name a few—and a commitment to reorganizing . . . society, so that the self development of people can take precedence over imperialism, economic expansion and material desires. (as quoted in Houston, 1996, p. 217)

Given the scope of the problem and the need for taking action, it might be wise to take Ruether's (1992) advice that we hold a long-term view into the future:

> Our revolution is not just for us, but for our children, for the generations of living beings to come. What we can do is to plant a seed, nurture a seed-bearing plant here and there, and hope for a harvest that goes beyond the limits of our powers and the span of our lives. (pp. 273–274)

MOVING BEYOND TO ECO-FEMINISM

An educational leader who seeks a viable and sustaining vision for the future needs to include all voices, those of women as well as men, those of different classes, racial-ethnicities, sexual orientations, religious diversities, and more. To do so, Fasching and deChant (2001) propose moving beyond feminism and its limitations toward a model that combines ecology and feminism, called eco-feminism.

The authors begin with the assumption that each life exists within a complex social ecology consisting of one's family, friendships, work life, associations, and civic and religious communities. Each of these spheres forms a social-institutional context, which holds an implicit set of expectations, values, and beliefs that make up its morality. For example, a school administrator might be a daughter, wife, painter, Rotarian, golfer, and Catholic. All of these different social contexts contribute to an understanding of good and evil, right and wrong, and positive and negative. Each social context may have a set of implicit expectations about what makes a good person, be it a daughter, a spouse, or a school administrator. We maintain a multiplicity of personalities that address our different social contexts.

> I am a different person with my family than I am with my boss, and different still with my friends, and so on. Each of the social environments we enter—work, family, friendship, voluntary associations, political movements, religious communities, etc.—require us to be a different person. And every one of the social roles we embrace in constructing our social identities has a story or complex of stories attached to it, which we consciously or unconsciously absorb. (Fasching & deChant, 2001, p. 303)

In leading an ethical life, the challenge is to fulfill the myriad of expectations placed upon us in each context. Parents know this challenge when they are forced to juggle work responsibilities and a sick child. The stress can be even greater with a long-term illness of a child or family member.

According to Fasching and deChant (2001), maintaining these multiplicities is possible through our capacity to "double." This process involves alienating our own selves, what the authors call "secondary doubling." It can be useful as we are able to see our actions objectively and reflect upon them. But secondary doubling can be problematic when we are not personally connected with what we do. In bureaucratic organizations like school systems, we are often compartmentalized within roles and responsibilities. Someone at the top decides to take a particular action directed toward a particular end. Without necessarily questioning the decision, we follow orders as we are directed. In ordinary circumstances, such action may be considered routine, but at its extremes, the "secondary doubling" can alienate us from our best ethical behavior.

Parker Palmer (2004) relates a story about a government bureaucrat who was experiencing painful conflicts between his values and power politics. It happened at a retreat that Palmer led in Washington, DC.

> One participant had worked for a decade in the U.S. Department of Agriculture, after farming for twenty-five years in northeastern Iowa. On his desk at that moment was a proposal related to the preservation of midwestern topsoil, which is being depleted at a rapid rate by agribusiness practices that value short term profits over the well-being of the earth. His "farmer's heart," he kept saying, knew how the proposal should be handled. But his political instincts warned him that following his heart would result in serious trouble, not least with his immediate superior.
>
> On the last morning of our gathering, the man from Agriculture, looking bleary-eyed, told us that it had become clear to him during a sleepless night that he needed to return to his office and follow his farmer's heart.
>
> After a thoughtful silence, someone asked him, "How will you deal with your boss, given his opposition to what you intend to do?"
>
> "It won't be easy," replied this farmer-turned-bureaucrat. "But during this retreat, I've remembered something important: I don't report to my boss. I report to the land." (Palmer, 2004, pp. 18–19)

Palmer cautions us that he does not know if the man did return to work and do as he resolved, but it was clear that he had validated what was most important to him. He tried to bring together his multiple selves, that of farmer, bureaucrat, citizen, and caretaker of the earth.

With eco-feminism, Fasching and deChant (2001) propose that we can attend to these multiple moral identities within our diverse social contexts. It validates the importance of diversity and reminds us that the greater the complexity present in life, the more likely is survival, a lesson learned from evolution.

> The more complexity there is in our social life (i.e., the more roles we must play in various social/institutional contexts), the more sensitive and life-sustaining our conscience will be. And conversely, the less complex and more simplified our social ecology becomes, the less sensitive and life-sustaining our conscience will be. (Fasching & deChant, 2001, p. 305)

Another way of looking at eco-feminism is through what Margaret Urban Walker (1998) calls "the structure of our responsibilities. . . . Specific moral claims on us arise from our contact or relationship with others whose interests are vulnerable to our actions and choices" (p. 107). Walker suggests applying an ethic of care but specifies that women need to rise above the bottomless pit of self-sacrifice and nurturing that denies their own personal integrity. She also notes that an ethic of personal integrity that denies empathy for others is equally unacceptable. Walker states, "Both [care and integrity] try to get the meanings, motives, commitments, and connections that move individuals through their distinctive lives into the right relations with morality's guiding and constraining force within those lives" (p. 108).

How might we accomplish such a balance? Virginia Held (1993) observes, "Since feminist approaches to morality are suspicious of rather than eager to offer highly abstract theories and simple principles, they are more likely to emphasize methods of moral inquiry and processes of moral improvement than to propound finished, comprehensive theories" (p. 219). Consider the example of a young man who reflected upon his work as a newly appointed elementary school principal. "You know, I recently became a dad, and it's changed how I think about my work. I mean, I wonder, what if this kid were my kid? How would I feel? I try to think about the parents' perspective more than ever before." In theory, the needs of a specific child should be cared about, but by turning inquiry on such care in a concrete way, this principal has moved beyond an abstract theory of care to one that maintains his own personal integrity while making the concept more real. It is theory that

Charlene Haddock Siegfried (1996) characterizes as "inquiry directed toward changing situations, preeminently social situations, which always include human participants" (p. 263).

Every social-institutional context confronts us with genuine ethical obligations toward others. It is possible to cultivate the awareness necessary to assume more than one identification and to see the world through more than one social context. This ecology of conscience is a relational-ecological model of justice, care, and personal integrity where the self is not set apart from others but moves in multiple social roles and across multiple contexts. As Fasching and deChant (2001) suggest,

> The ethical life and justice are fostered by nurturing the complexity of our social ecology. The more complexity there is, the more strangers enter into our life and the broader and more inclusive our ethical consciousness becomes. The ethical life requires more than just taking care of one's friends; it demands hospitality to the stranger (both human and non-human). (p. 307)

SUMMARY

Critiquing taken-for-granted ways of thinking, feminism presents us with an alternative perspective that informs our moral-ethical decisions in a way different from an ethic of justice and moral development. In this chapter, we took an in-depth look at feminist ethics and its fundamental tenets. We considered how feminism has been applied in three areas of study—equity, women's ways of knowing, and power. We looked at the various ways that feminism might inform our thinking as school administrators. In addition, we identified some of its limitations—as women's work, as essentialist, and as too theoretical. To move beyond these limitations, we proposed the more encompassing perspective of eco-feminism that recognizes the multiple contexts in which we live. It is a model of critique that is highly appropriate for engaging in democratic leadership.

Part II

METHODS

CHAPTER 5

John Dewey and Democratic Leadership

Throughout this book, we have built upon the premise that an ethic of democratic leadership—where leaders foster democratic practices in their institutions—is the most effective and desirable form of leadership available (Kramer, 2006a). We believe this for three reasons. First, like John Dewey, we see that the problems of any group or organization occur as people associate with one another. Conflict between individuals is inevitable, and if not handled wisely, it can debilitate the persons involved and even the organization. Democratic practices recognize this and guide how we ought to approach disputes and clashes. Second, Dewey's concept of democracy can be defined as the razor line of space between the needs of the individual and the needs of the group or groups to which the individual belongs. This means that effective leaders recognize the importance of balancing individual needs with group needs. Third, there are habitual behaviors in organizations that can restrict how we respond to complex problems. Democratic leaders can apply creativity and moral imagination to problems requiring new ways of doing things. In this chapter, we illustrate how democratic leadership might be enacted in the following case.

NANCY'S DILEMMA

Nancy is the dean of students at Garden Middle School in a large, suburban school district. Reluctantly, the school district joined a voluntary desegregation consortium with twelve other school districts. As a consequence, they began receiving a small but significant number of students of color who were bused in from the nearby metropolitan center. This has been a very different experience for the fairly homogeneous, upper-middle-class school district. The result of the busing has been heightened racial-ethnic tensions among the students, antagonism among some of the faculty, hostility from parents, and an ethical dilemma for Nancy.

As the dean of students, Nancy is responsible for all student concerns, from monitoring attendance to administering disciplinary actions. She must deal directly with the upsets caused by student misconduct inside the classroom as well as in the halls and the lunchroom. And at the middle school, adolescents often act out their frustrations. Nancy has also been deeply committed to ensuring educational equity and to promoting equal opportunity. As a white person, she has done volunteer work with minority communities in the urban center and has learned about the hardships that families in poverty face. In addition, her graduate studies in leadership and critical theories have helped her become more aware of the racial-ethnic tensions in her community and school.

Transported daily by bus into the district, these students of color are struggling to adapt to their new school environment. There is little integration between whites and students of color. The new students usually cluster together during recess and lunch. Some have taken on a "don't mess with me" attitude that has led to fights among the students. But teachers seem to see only the students of color as being at fault. For example, once while Nancy was walking the hall, two eighth-grade boys, one black and one white, came bounding up to her. "Are you coming to the basketball game tonight?" they asked breathlessly. Before she could respond, a classroom teacher came out of his room and dressed down the black student for wearing saggy pants. Nancy was shocked. The white student also had on saggy pants, and the teacher said nothing to him, yet he went out of his way to address the black student.

When Nancy raised these concerns with the faculty, teachers accused her of taking the side of the new students, even if that was not the case. Many of these teachers have more years of seniority than she has at Garden Middle School, and they can make life difficult for anyone with a different point of view. Having spent years teaching a traditional secondary school curriculum, many teachers retain habits that have worked in the past, but they are being challenged with this new group of students. They have also had little in the way of training and support for differentiated instruction. Some are already grumbling about how these "new kids" will bring the school's test scores down.

Nancy is in a similar bind with the parents. The Voluntary Desegregation Plan allows parents outside the district to choose to send their kids to Garden Middle School. Understandably, it is a difficult choice to send one's children to another school district across town, requiring long bus rides each day. In making this choice, parents sought assurances from the school that their children would receive the same quality of education, or better, at their neighborhood schools. Now some parents are frustrated by the school's lack of sensitivity to their children's needs. The administration and teachers seem to have little experience with minority students and are hardly welcoming. Almost all communication from the school to the parents raises their anxiety level even further. When Nancy contacted some parents, they asked blunt questions and made emotional demands on behalf of their children. In one case, when a new student got into a fight, the parent demanded that the school *not* implement the standard procedure of a three-day suspension. But Nancy felt that she had no choice in the matter, and the parent called her a "racist white cracker." While hurt over the remark, she could understand the parent's concerns. If the kids were put out of school so easily, and school was not where they wanted to be in the first place, then the suspension seemed to achieve the wrong outcome. It might also place an economic burden on a family already having difficulty making ends meet.

For his part, the school principal is too busy to deal with these matters. He has been frequently off campus at district meetings and has left things for Nancy to handle on her own. His major concern has centered on the federal mandate of No Child Left Behind and on retaining his school's record of sterling academic achievement. There is a chance that Garden Middle might fall below par, and that would get his attention right away.

Nancy is in a very uncomfortable ethical position. As the dean of students, she needs to deal fairly and consistently with all of the students at Garden Middle. It is part of her obligation as an administrator. For some on the faculty, this means enforcing strong rules that are applied in the same way for every student, regardless of circumstance. But her obligation is also to care for the needs of these new students, ensuring that they make a good transition to Garden Middle. It might entail providing interventions that are more appropriate and equitable for them, even though they are in the minority. This action would be aligned with her deep personal commitment to ensuring equal educational opportunity.

CONDITIONS CALLING FOR DEMOCRATIC LEADERSHIP

Nancy's case illustrates the three main conditions that call for democratic leadership, as well as how ethical dilemmas occur in schools. Let's look at how each condition plays out in this particular situation. First, we consider the three problems of association that create conflict, as noted by Dewey. Next, we look at balancing the needs of individuals with the needs of the groups to which they belong. And finally, we explore and deconstruct habitual behaviors among the school members in order to resolve Nancy's ethical dilemma.

PROBLEMS OF ASSOCIATION

Dewey saw conflict as an inevitable part of human society. He noted that human beings make demands on each other, and these demands are sometimes at odds with what individuals wish to do. Calling these conflicts "problems of association," Dewey and Tufts (1932a) categorized them in terms of (1) social order conflicts ("class and mass"), where a dominant group, be it social, political, or economic, seeks to maintain its hegemonic position with regard to groups that are hierarchically or socially nondominant; (2) change conflicts ("old versus new," "conservative versus liberal"), where the old order wishes to preserve its forms while a new order seeks to establish different forms of association and organization; and (3) private versus public conflicts, where private voluntary solutions come into conflict with public agency solutions (pp. 325–327).

Social Order Conflicts

In terms of hierarchy in school organizations, classroom teachers generally report to their administrator. The principal is often solely responsible for hiring, supervising, and evaluating the teachers and staff in a school. In turn, principals are usually hired and evaluated by their superior. This could be the superintendent of the district or a designee like the deputy in charge of schools. A superintendent might be hired and appointed by a school board. The organizational hierarchy is clearly delineated between teacher and principal, between principal and superintendent, and between superintendent and school board. Often, what is not so clear is how parents, community leaders, and business leaders figure into the social order. In some schools and districts, these groups may exert considerable influence on what policies are enacted and how schools are supported. In other cases, they may have very little influence on what happens at school, or they may act simply to reinforce the administrator's wishes.

In her position as dean of students, Nancy is specifically responsible for monitoring the academic and social welfare of each student at Garden Middle. Her position is also one of support services. She is neither a teacher nor the administrator in charge. In a way, she is at the same hierarchical level as the classroom teachers, since she does not directly supervise them and has no authority over them. Yet she must work with them on matters of discipline and student conduct, often communicating their concerns to the parents. She serves as a go-between for the parents and the school. Ultimately, she must answer to the principal, as he has the final say on all matters of student conduct. She is also subject to his review and appraisal of her performance of her duties and responsibilities.

Examining potential social order conflicts, we note that Garden Middle School is situated within a school district in the state. The principal reports to his boss, the district's superintendent, and as such, the principal must deal with district matters that have taken him away from the school. Further, he must attend to the federal mandates of No Child Left Behind, ensuring that his school meets the standards and achievement benchmarks required by the state. It is likely that his performance as school principal will be assessed based upon whether he is successful in doing so. Using the category of social order conflicts, we can consider how a school exists within a complex organization and how its leadership must respond not only to constituents like parents but also to state and national expectations for success.

Change Conflicts

Conflicts occur between the old and the new. One group seeks to preserve what has been before and might hold that school traditions are at
stake if change is enacted. The other group seeks to do things differently, possibly in better and more progressive ways. However, those
newer ways have not been tested, and the group advocating change
struggles to assert its influence on the organization. As Machiavelli
wrote in *The Prince*, "Nothing is more dangerous or difficult than introducing a new order of things" (quoted in Badaracco, 2006, p. 76).
Dewey recognized that old-versus-new conflicts take on a larger meaning than just that of conserving the past versus adopting new forms for
the future. The past is seen as socially organized, in that it is a known
way that has led to stability for the group. The future is nebulous and is
therefore disorganized in the minds of the persons involved. The proposed new forms have no credibility and are viewed skeptically, sometimes even fearfully, by those who are well entrenched in the organization. One further complication is that those who stand to gain the most
from new forms may have little power or resources under the current
system. They may be suspicious of the existing organizational structure
since their experience of organizations is one of lacking resources
(Dewey & Tufts, 1932a).

In the case study, Garden Middle School is operating under its old
habits and routines. Students who attend the school have been mostly
white and affluent, coming directly from the suburban community.
They have grown up with Garden Middle's way of doing things. According to some of the faculty and staff, the existing rules and routines
have worked in the past and should work now. Some teachers are concerned that if they change their approach, they will water down their
curricular standards. But with the new group of students, things are not
working. The new students bring different academic and social backgrounds, along with different needs, desires, and expectations. This
does not mean that school rules don't apply, but it does mean that there
will be conflict between the old and new cultures. Rarely does the
forced juxtaposition of two cultures go smoothly without conflicts and
clashes. In this case, there are racial-ethnic as well as class differences
to add to the mix. Teachers have not had to deal with these kinds of differences; neither have they been given training or support in delivering

differentiated instruction to serve the newer students. They may resort to habitual ways of doing things that will not work with the new challenges and different needs that the new students bring.

Nancy is concerned that if a change is not made in the way the school approaches the new students, they will be lost, or worse, they will act out their frustration in destructive ways. However, her concerns have little credibility with many of the senior faculty because the students represent an unknown future that is of questionable value. As well, Nancy has made limited inroads with the parents because, as school personnel, she is viewed distrustfully. Thus, the ethical conflict of conserving old forms versus introducing newer ways is evident in Nancy's situation.

Private-Public Conflict

This type of conflict is present whenever private interests and public agency clash. Nancy has "private interests" in that she wants the new students to succeed. Individual students and their parents also have "private interests" to ensure that their needs are met. As a public agency, the school has shared or mutually agreed-upon ways of resolving conflict, which are present in the rules, regulations, and policies that are in place. These may or may not be appropriate to the situation at hand. For example, Nancy desires that the discipline rules be individually adjusted to meet what she perceives to be the specific needs of the students involved. However, in the interest of equal treatment, the Garden Middle School faculty want the school rules to be upheld in a consistent manner. For them, this would be fair and just. By doing so, they are upholding the public agency of the school. At the same time, the faculty and staff probably do not want the school to be thought of as uncaring or even racist. This negative image can become a mechanism for leverage by Nancy and the parents as they negotiate this conflict.

BALANCING INDIVIDUAL AND GROUP NEEDS

The second condition calling for democratic leadership is that the needs of individuals and the needs of groups often conflict. While we have touched upon this condition in discussing problems of association, there is a more specific way to point to problems that arise between individuals and groups. To paraphrase Dewey, leadership dilemmas are not so much between individuals as between groups of individuals conflicting over some larger idea or social order. Such conflicts can be personalized at the individual level. When things do not go our way, we tend to seek out a cause that is much more personal or individualized: "He doesn't like me," or "The teacher always picks on me." However, rarely does just one person feel the fallout from any given conflict. So what appears to be a conflict between individuals probably relates to the group.

As the students of color became frustrated with Garden Middle School teachers, they began to act out by fighting with the white students. While these were individual acts on the part of the students, they had taken on racial overtones. In one case, Nancy felt that she had no choice but to implement a three-day suspension on a black student for fighting. The parent responded by calling Nancy a racist and by viewing the actions of the school as those of a racist institution. Nancy began to fear that the parents would create a public spectacle that could negatively affect the entire school community. In a similar way, the teachers enlarged the incident by viewing it as a threat to the academic integrity of Garden Middle. The combination of the academic integrity issue and the racial tensions dramatically changed the situation. What had been students who manifested their own internal conflicts by fighting became a conflict between a group of school personnel defending their school's high academic standards and a group of irate parents objecting to its racism.

John Dewey felt that the greatest challenge of democracy was balancing the individual needs of community members with the overall needs of the community group. He proposed a test for whether the needs of the individual or the group were out of balance. Dewey believed that the role of any group was to support its members' self-actualization. At the same time, the growth of any individual should not get in the way of the group's ability to support its members' individual growth. While the test seems simple, it is actually quite complicated. How are individual needs to be determined? To what extent does one individual represent the group as a whole? How are roles defined for individuals and groups?

How does the leader monitor what is occurring? Who determines whether a threshold is reached that tips the equation toward one side or the other?

What are some of the individual and group needs present in Nancy's situation? The students of color need to find success and acceptance in their new school—a building that feels hostile to them. Their parents need to feel that the school is treating their children fairly while providing a quality educational environment for them. The faculty and staff believe that their professional integrity is tied to enforcing rules and regulations consistently. Many also believe that their academic standards are being challenged and that they need to be able to respond effectively to meet all of their students' needs. Garden Middle School as a whole school community needs to operate in an orderly and safe manner. Hopefully they will seek to provide a caring school environment as well as a rigorous academic one. Nancy needs to feel that she is advancing equitable treatment and bettering the lot of all her students. She needs to consider all students at Garden Middle, not only the newest ones. She also needs to be supported by the school administrator responsible for the school. Though balancing these needs will not be easy, recognizing what is demanded and what is at stake marks the start of working the dilemma.

HABITUAL RESPONSES

The third condition of social interaction that calls for democratic leadership is habitual responses on the part of members, leaders, and the organization. Identifying this condition may seem unnecessary in light of the discussion about change conflicts as one of the problems of association. However, with change conflicts, the parties on either side are consciously seeking either to conserve the old ways or to redefine new ways to respond. Both sides are aware of what they are advocating and why they want either constancy or change. In the case of habitual responses, members may not be aware of their behaviors or actions.

Habits and routines are everyday behaviors that form standard ways of doing things, frequently taken for granted and often unconsciously executed (Conley & Enomoto, 2005). In school organizations, habitual activities can include how class attendance is taken, how courses are scheduled each year, or how personnel are routinely evaluated. Dewey suggests that habitual responses serve us well in that we do not have to think about performing these behaviors, thus freeing us to attend to other matters. But habits can also stifle members' behavior, curb innovation, and structure decision making when problems occur. They may persist when they are no longer necessary or appropriate because particular external pressures exist or because internal constraints limit change (Feldman, 1988). Individuals and groups might also resist making any changes. Routines in organizations may even restrict our ways of defining problems and seeking solutions.

In the Garden Middle School case, Nancy recognizes the inadequacy of the school's habitual responses to the students from the metropolitan center. Seeking to do business as usual, many faculty members appear to be unaware of the challenges of the new situation. Their successes in the past might blind them as to how to deal with students who bring different needs to Garden Middle. Likewise, the parents of the new students might be operating out of habitual responses to institutional and societal racism. For both groups, parents and teachers, the responses could be unconsciously executed.

For Nancy, negotiating the space between the school and parents is complicated for several reasons. First, she is a well-educated white woman who is aware of the privilege conferred by her class and race. She believes that most of her colleagues at Garden Middle do not recognize their own privilege, either socioeconomic or otherwise. Second, Nancy can identify aspects of racism at Garden Middle School based on her six years there. She might also contribute to it even if she believes that racism is wrong and fights to overcome it. To the parents, she represents the school and may be viewed negatively because of it. Third, Nancy is aware that Garden Middle School has operated successfully for more than 25 years in terms of academic achievement. She is confronting a long-standing habitual way of doing things ("the Garden Middle School way") that has been appropriate and successful. Perhaps individual student conflicts and external pressures from parents and community have not pushed Garden Middle beyond its habitual responses.

DEMOCRACY AND DEMOCRATIC LEADERSHIP

We have been using the term *democracy* throughout this chapter, and even throughout this book. Now it is time to show how democratic leadership addresses conflicts that are related to the problems of association mentioned above and are faced constantly in a pluralistic school organization.

In writing about democracy, Dewey did not necessarily mean a government form (e.g., three separate branches of government) or a political form (e.g., free elections, voter representation). Rather, the term was more about living in association with others. "A democracy is more than a form of government; it is primarily a mode of associated living, of conjoint communicated experience" (Dewey, 1916, p. 87). An overarching metaethic, democracy guides how we ought to approach living with each other. Dewey saw the true measure of democracy as the discursive, dialogical quality between individuals and groups, and their mutual growth, which makes democracy viable on a daily basis.

Recall that in chapter 1 we spoke of democracy as a way of negotiating the potential growth of the individual with the needs of the group and vice versa. Negotiation can lead to individual development as well as achievement of the group's purpose. To do this, individuals must take a responsible share in providing direction for the group's activities.

> From the standpoints of the groups, [democracy] demands liberation of the potentialities of members of a group in harmony with the interests and goods which are common. Since every individual is a member of many groups, this specification cannot be fulfilled except when different groups interact flexibly and fully in connection with other groups. (Dewey, 1916, p. 147)

Dewey saw the need for conscious sharing among members and the free association among differing groups. He believed that this kind of exchange would promote individual as well as group development and progress.

Dewey understood that individuals are members of many social groups and that communication is essential to fulfilling individual potential. Thus, he believed that the "communicated experience" is key to achieving democratic ends. What did he mean by communicated experience? Dewey (1916) suggested the following as illustrative:

> Try the experiment of communicating, with fullness and accuracy, some experience to another, especially if it be somewhat complicated, and you will find your own attitude toward your experience changing; otherwise you resort to expletives and ejaculations. The experience has to be formulated in order to be communicated. To formulate requires getting outside of it, seeing it as another would see it, considering what points of contact it has with the life of another so that it may be got into such form that he can appreciate its meaning. (pp. 9–10)

In the social endeavor of communicating with others, Dewey identified processes of reconsideration, revision, meaning making, and ultimately education. "When communication occurs, all natural events are the subject of reconsideration and revision; they are re-adapted to meet the requirements of conversation, whether it be public discourse or that preliminary discourse termed thinking" (Dewey, 1938, p. 166).

Accordingly, the link between communication and democracy cannot be overstated. Democracy "demand[s] *communication* [italics in original] as a prerequisite" (Dewey, 1927, p. 152), for "society not only continues to exist *by* transmission, *by* communication, but it may fairly be said to exist *in* transmission, *in* communication [italics in original]" (Dewey, 1916, p. 4). By communicating with one another, we create our societies. We construct social groups, their meanings, and their identities through our words, symbols, and actions. We specify our membership and define who we are in association with our group affiliations. Only if the communication is open, sharing, and grounded in truth seeking, can we begin to form social structures that can handle the diverse needs of our society. Dewey believed that democracy required this kind of communication in order to thrive.

Dewey advocated that we communicate in a way that makes each of us refer our actions to the beliefs, needs, and actions of others. In other words, we must "get outside our own experience" and relate to the other's perspectives and experiences. For example, if Nancy approaches her dilemma from a democratic ethic, she must begin to understand the diverse perspectives presented by the students, parents, teachers, and principal. She needs to start by listening to them. It seems a logical first step but will not be easy because she has already taken a position and might not appear to be open to some teachers or parents. Getting outside her own experience might mean suspending her judgments and refraining from voicing an opinion. The emphasis will be on understanding the other person's needs and desires in the situation. By listening to their heartfelt concerns, she will be able to see more comprehensively what is needed for the school. Nancy will also need to communicate between groups and might get people to listen to each other. For now, the lines are so clearly delineated that there can only be winners and losers. How can she address this challenge when clearly she is in a very difficult and tenuous position? For this, Dewey would suggest the use of moral imagination.

MORAL IMAGINATION

Nancy's situation calls into question which group is right. Is it the parents or the teachers? Taking the approach that one side is right and the other is wrong, Nancy will most certainly fail to serve either group. She needs to understand the parents' concerns as well as gain their trust in working for their children's best interests. She also needs to encourage the teachers to work with her, connecting with those who might be supportive as well as listening carefully to those who might oppose her perspective. If teachers need more support and professional development, how could she provide that? If Nancy sees the parents' and teachers' concerns as mutually exclusive, then she will not be able to influence the sides toward a positive outcome. She will need to find the common ground that can unite them while doing some creative problem solving to respond to the situation at hand. In addition to excellent communication skills, she will need to employ a more creative set of skills and be morally imaginative.

Stephen Fesmire (2003), a scholar of John Dewey, states that there are two main themes in Dewey's moral imagination. The first is "empathetic projection," where one imagines the other person's "aspirations, interests, and worries as our own" (p. 65). Dewey began with empathy in order to discern what it would be like to be the other, rather than superimposing one's views upon others. The second theme relates to moral imagination as a tool or skill set for yielding good ends. This might involve the skill of asking pertinent yet challenging questions, or of facilitating discussions with individuals or groups to determine what is most desired. It could also be about rehearsing consequences that might be likely given certain actions or strategies. In summarizing the two themes, Fesmire states that "imagination in Dewey's central sense is the capacity to concretely perceive what is before us in light of what could be" (p. 65).

Demonstrating moral imagination as a leader is not easy. It involves working the process toward uncertain ends, negotiating the space between different and often clashing groups, and demonstrating bold action and moral courage. It requires patience, commitment, and determination. Dewey points out that imaginative persons are often condemned for their ideas. Only later might their ideas be acknowledged and possibly recognized as beneficial. Because of this, exercising moral imagination may feel futile or fanciful. However, if we are to truly negotiate the vast range of different needs and perceptions in our society, we must be morally imaginative and promote the kind of creative thinking necessary. In essence, moral imagination can ensure that the requirements of democratic ethics are met.

BACK TO THE CASE

Facing an ethical dilemma, Nancy recognizes that she is responsible for upholding the policies and procedures of the district, whether they are the products of privilege or not. This is why the "racist" accusation stung her so hard. She feels like a racist in this situation. Privately, she wonders why she cannot address the issues underlying the conflicts taking place and why it is not possible to affect the rules in a way that is more cognizant of the needs of the new students and their families. She sees the faculty group taking precedence over individuals in this situation because of habit. On the other hand, the teachers see any attempt to treat the children differently as being ultimately harmful. Both parents and teachers see Nancy as part of the problem because she seeks to uphold the old order as well as question it.

Yet Nancy has numerous tools that can be imaginatively used. At her disposal is the ability to bring people together. She can lead all participants through creative processes that imagine different strategies for addressing the situation, and the possible outcomes. She can encourage empathy and model listening actively. Or she can rely on the habits of old. So far, habits have gotten her into a conflict, where winners take all and losers may literally be left behind. Democratic ethics demand that she question habitual responses and encourage the imaginative. Dewey (1916) observes,

> The extension in space of the number of individuals who participate in an interest so that each has to refer his own action to that of others, and to consider the action of others to give point and direction to his own, is equivalent of the breaking down of those barriers of class, race, and national territory which kept men from perceiving the full import of their activity. (p. 87)

In other words, Dewey saw in 1916 the import of morally imaginative action toward the goal of a more equitable social order.

SUMMARY

In this chapter, Dewey's ethic of democratic leadership was proposed as an effective means to engage with others and strive toward collaboration. Key to developing democratic leadership is identifying three conditions calling for democracy and employing appropriate tools to facilitate it. Dewey proposed that we identify problems of association (social order, change, and private versus public conflicts); balance individual and group needs; and become aware of habitual responses to problems. Nancy's ethical dilemma at Garden Middle School is used as a case study for considering these three conditions.

Throughout this chapter, we have advocated for democracy as an overarching metaethic that guides how to approach the ethical dilemmas occurring in association with each other. It promotes negotiating for the potential growth of individuals within the context of their groups. It values communicating openly and freely to understand the needs and concerns of all. It advises exercising moral imagination, boldness, and courage to address the complex issues of multifaceted social groups. In chapter 6, we explore more completely an inquiry method for this kind of democratic leadership.

An Inquiry Method for
Working Ethical Dilemmas

In this chapter, we present an inquiry method for negotiating and working through the ethical dilemmas that leaders face in their educational settings. The method was developed through our observation of and practical experiences with leaders. Over the past three years, it has become a linchpin for a doctoral ethics course in which students examine their values and beliefs, analyze their leadership challenges from an ethical standpoint, and apply principles as they work through the solutions. Working the method has led our students to both personal and professional growth in understanding themselves and the challenges they face.

The method is directly informed by John Dewey's notions of democracy and democratic practices. As we have argued in chapter 5, democracy is the appropriate metaethic to respond to the diverse needs of individuals and groups, particularly as they clash with one another. This is the work that our school leaders must engage in as they negotiate and try to resolve ethical dilemmas. They need to be able to inquire and investigate problems with openness and honesty, communicating freely with the parties involved. They need to know how to systematically reflect upon intended actions and likely consequences for the youngsters within their care. Ultimately, their work involves caring for all of the students in their schools.

We also draw from Stephen Fesmire's (2003) application of moral imagination in working creatively toward meaningful and relevant solutions. While imagination and creativity might lead to painful conclusions, Fesmire contends that it is far better to face situations honestly than to pretend otherwise. "What is most at stake in moral life is not some quantifiable pleasure or pain, but 'what kind of person one is to become' and what kind of world is to develop. These questions are explored in imagination" (p. 76).

Dewey's democratic practices and Fesmire's moral imagination provide the grounding for this inquiry method. To describe it more fully, we first clarify the meaning of an ethical dilemma, as this determines whether one would commit the resources necessary to such an endeavor. We also consider how to define the method's usefulness. We propose that an inquiry method for ethical deliberation needs two critical components, discernment and action, in order for leaders to negotiate skillfully toward resolution. These components are found in the four phases of the method, and we illustrate the phases in a case of a struggling organization.

DEFINING AN ETHICAL DILEMMA

It is important to clarify what we mean by an ethical dilemma. For some people, the term *dilemma* refers to a problem that has multiple choices of equal value. For example, in trying to hire a new teacher, we may need to choose between two equally qualified candidates. There are two good choices so that no matter what decision is made, the school gains a qualified teacher. But suppose that the choice is between two very different teacher applicants, where selecting one over the other will negatively affect one school program or another. Certain youngsters might be significantly affected by the hiring decision. No matter what decision is made, it feels like a lose-lose situation. Here the case becomes an ethical dilemma where the choices might not be optimal or might require compromise among all involved.

Most problems of practice can be interpreted as dilemmas, particularly if multiple persons are involved in the deliberation. This can complicate how decisions are made. As the leader of the organization, your dilemma may not be in deciding what you think the right course is. Rather, you must assist people representing multiple perspectives to come to some form of agreement where no one is absolutely thrilled with any of the options available. Some leaders have worked this out by making many of the decisions themselves. While this minimizes some deliberative angst if the dilemma is sufficiently contentious, it may create other problems such as feelings that the leader does not listen or that she stifles other points of view.

In addition, a dilemma can be truly complex because of its unique context and cast of characters. For example, you may find yourself faced with the teacher selection problem described above, but if you have faced it many times, you may have worked out an approach to resolving the situation. It becomes less a dilemma than a tough decision that you handle as part of the job. Rushworth Kidder (1995) refers to this in distinguishing between a tough decision, one that you do not like making but know must be made, and a dilemma, where the problem has multiple choices of equal but differing value. However, if it is your first time and you have not thought through the implications of the problem—the effects on students, faculty, and staff, and possibly on parents and the community—then the complexity of the problem may seem to be quite messy and nebulous.

In short, the nature of a dilemma is in the complexity of the choices it offers, the deliberation related to values of right and wrong, and the judgments that one must make as a result of such choices. What might be a small problem to resolve for one person may be a tough decision for someone else. There might also be individuals or groups polarized over the issues, as in Nancy's case in chapter 5. Or there might be larger social issues or political contexts that create more tensions in resolving the situation. The relative experience of the leadership, the perspectives of the varied participants, and the cultural context all affect working the dilemma. These factors force us to probe for deeper understanding of the unique context of the situation.

DEFINING A USEFUL METHOD

Our work with leaders struggling through ethical dilemmas points out the need for more than reflection and self-illumination. How does a leader step beyond reflecting about one's values and recognize diverse perspectives? How can a leader take concerted action toward resolving the situation and actually lead others? We believe that the answer actually lies in the question. Leaders need a method of inquiry that is both reflective and active, that acknowledges the complexity of ethical dilemmas, and that fits within the kind of work that leaders need to do in order to be effective. But we have seen many methods through our research and teaching that are so complicated that we are not inclined to use them. Alternatively, there are methods that constrain creative and progressive thinking. Those, too, are inadequate for problem solving and decision making. We believe there is a need for a systematic yet dynamic way to sort through the often chaotic situations that create ethical dilemmas.

To be useful, a method for ethical inquiry must meet four criteria. First, we believe that the method needs to be exploratory, taking into account as much as can be known about any given situation. Anything and everything might be viewed as data—multiple perspectives, people's feelings, historical precedents, cultural rituals and routines, rules, regulations, and resources. In short, anything that relates to the problem needs to be considered. The method should also explore meaning. Why is the situation important? What does it mean to the individuals involved? In general, the method must enable a leader to candidly describe the situation as it truly is and not as one might want it to be.

Second, no dilemma or problem remains static over time. New information arises, old information becomes less credible, different perspectives become available, and people's views evolve. We believe that the method must be able to accommodate these changes, reflecting the dynamic nature of the process. This also means that the method is iterative. Faced with complex dilemmas, we might work toward partial resolution, returning again and again as other factors play out.

Third, we see moral imagination as integral to the method, from identifying the problem through resolving it. But we do not see moral imagination as moral permissiveness. Imagination and creativity can foster a permissive ("almost anything goes") culture as long as the consequences are desirable. Recall our discussion of ethical tensions in chapter 2. Nothing could be further from our purpose. Identifying duties and virtues to which leaders and followers feel loyalty is a major part of moral imagination, and this recognition offers a check on rampant consequentialism.

Fourth, we believe that the method should result in a strengthening of participants' capacity for moral action and the group's capacity for growth. If growth is not expected as a result of an approach to dilemmas, then such methods are very limited in their use. What good is it to continue to rehash the same problems of practice if we do not get better at working them? If we are to become more effective at working with people, then we need to develop our capacity as democratic leaders, meaning the promotion of others' well-being. This goes for individuals, groups, and whole organizations.

DISCERNMENT AND ACTION

Based upon inquiry, the method that we propose moves synergistically back and forth from processes of discernment and analysis to imaginative action. It is an act that pragmatists describe as "experimental" because both antecedents and consequential factors need to be considered. Antecedents contextualize the problem, while consequences help us rehearse the various possible effects of any action, even before these effects take place. The processes of discernment and action make for the dynamic, iterative method of inquiry.

For our purposes, the term *discernment* means engaging in reflection to bring about personal or group understanding and clarity. Sometimes gaining clarity may be incremental as the facts of the case emerge in piecemeal fashion. It may also involve moments of insight or inspiration, those ahas that come after much deliberation and reflection to make sense out of the situation. In either case, discernment may be thought of as more of an internal process, whereas action is more overt and external.

When we speak of action, we mean behaviors that can be observed by others. Whereas discernment happens as participants engage in thinking through their own perceptions, action occurs when those perceptions are shared or when the whole group becomes more cognizant of a course or strategy to be taken. Action involves doing something to move the dilemma forward, be it seeking input from others or communicating about issues or concerns.

We illustrate how the processes of discernment and action work in tandem in the following case about an organization struggling to make music and make its payroll.

SPCO'S DILEMMA

Over the years, the St. Paul Chamber Orchestra (SPCO), a well-known and highly respected professional ensemble of 30 musicians, has managed to make its financial obligations, sometimes barely and sometimes profitably. However, after the departure of its longtime music director Hugh Wolfe, the SPCO was faced with the problem of finding a new music director and the accompanying financial dilemma of such a search. The SPCO board, the overall governing body of the SPCO, needed to decide whether to hire a "big name" director to attract season ticket holders, but that might be too expensive for the orchestra. Alternatively, they could hire a relatively unknown conductor for the position and keep within their budget.

For two years, the board struggled with this decision: either hire a well-known music director or build a reputation for an up-and-coming maestro. As defined, the problem led them to one conclusion—that the SPCO needed a music director. And why shouldn't this be? They had always had a music director. With this determined and with finances considered, the board decided to hire a new conductor from an even smaller ensemble. Unfortunately, the individual did not generate the kind of excitement the board had hoped. Failing to attract the public's interest with the new conductor, the SPCO's financial situation continued to worsen. By the end of the first year of the director's contract, there was a huge operating budget deficit.

The SPCO case exemplifies Dewey's observation that people do not usually accept facts that contradict their previously held views. He noted that we construct a habitual reality that may have served us well up to the present situation. The SPCO board could only see the solution in terms of affording to hire a new music director. That habitual response restricted their possibilities and pushed them into a situation that was financially worse. Only then were they forced to consider alternatives and initiate a new response.

To arrive at an ethical solution, leaders must be willing to examine and critique their own views with as much scrutiny as they give to others. Critical to such an examination is the leader's attitude, that openness and willingness to model self-scrutiny while asking the same of all other participants. This attitude promotes the necessary investigation and analysis of the problem. It takes a situation from describing what is, in terms of protecting one's perceptions, to describing what is, in terms of seeking the most accurate and agreed-upon description. Such reflection also raises questions that most leaders face in tough situations. What information should be shared? Is there a need to restrict some information? Might there be potential damage to others or negative consequences resulting from sharing everything? The leadership needs to reflect on when and how to share information to promote openness while not causing harm.

Once the SPCO musicians became aware of the financial situation, they immediately perceived the possibility of layoffs and of part-timers playing with the group. This would have been a disaster for them. Chamber orchestras are finely tuned ensembles in which the members get to know each other's artistic musicianship so well that they can predict musical possibilities and challenges in playing each score. They develop a unified sense of what to do in any piece of music. Suppose that, embarrassed at not resolving the SPCO's financial problems, the board had kept the operating deficit a secret from the musicians until the problem could no longer be hidden. The long-term effects on the orchestra would have been devastating. The more that information can be shared, and the more that people can freely discuss it, the better the possibility that the situation can be worked and satisfactorily resolved.

At some point in the dilemma, the process of discernment must shift toward taking action. In our inquiry method, actions are suggested in each of the method's four phases, so timing can be discerned in an ongoing manner. Once there is knowledge of desired outcomes, then actions can be plotted and carried out. Our experience is that specific actions toward problem solving are usually embedded within the dilemma itself and thus are informed by the continuous process of discernment. In the SPCO case, the orchestra players chose to hold their professional group together by taking a 20% pay cut to meet the SPCO's financial obligations. Other orchestras facing the same situation might have chosen a different course of action. Embedded in the SPCO was the culture of a chamber group—a small, intimate ensemble of specifically trained musicians. Such groups are not made up of interchangeable parts. Further, the long-term relationship among the players had developed expertise and camaraderie that bonded them together. For the SPCO, the

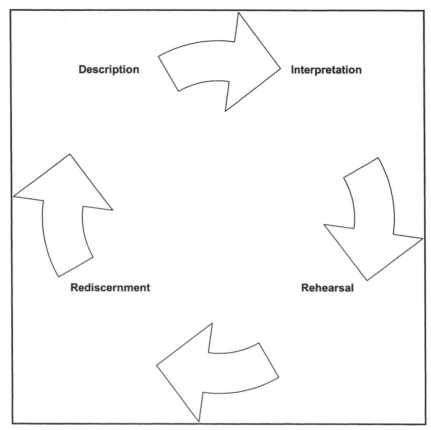

Figure 6.1.   The DIRR Method

act of taking a pay cut, while not desirable, became the preferable option to breaking up the orchestra.

Appropriate actions become clearer as information is shared, and
sometimes these actions can also point to the complexity of a situation
when multiple viewpoints are taken into account. However, since new
information changes the context of the dilemma, one can never think of
the situation as being totally resolved. Rather, we prefer to think of it
as working the dilemma and remaining open to changing our assumptions, perceptions, and contexts as information becomes available.
Once actions are discerned and agreed upon, a new cycle of further inquiry can be initiated. The method progresses from description and reflection to action and cycles back again. This leads us to the specific

components of our method, to which we give the acronym DIRR—*De*-scription, *I*nterpretation, *R*ehearsal, *R*ediscernment (see figure 6.1).

D = DESCRIPTION

As in qualitative research methods, the first step in working any ethical dilemma is description, which includes specifying the problem or situation, the environment in which it is located, and each person's involvement in what Fesmire calls "tangles of lived experience" (2003, p. 28). By this, Fesmire points out that description is not only a singular activity, but rather one in which multiple interpretations may be present. By fully describing the dilemma and reflecting upon one's personal involvement in it, individual's values and beliefs surface. This investigation could uncover what might be deeply rooted beliefs about right and wrong, factors related to the cultural norms of the group, and habitual responses that have been taken for granted.

What kinds of information should go into describing the dilemma? Include as much detail as possible, such as who is involved, what has occurred, when and where, and so on. These kinds of data lay the foundation for the first stage of the investigation before the next analytical stage. Description is more about the facts as the different participants see them, and it behooves all participants to acknowledge that the facts as they are known by each participant may not actually line up exactly. It is precisely with this type of task that the leader is crucial. Acknowledging different perceptions as a normal part of the process, the leader can begin to uncover the multiple interpretations of the situation as well as possible resolutions to be considered.

We encourage the leader to strive toward describing the dilemma in as rich a language as possible, with each participant invited to contribute and not constrained to holding back. In the SPCO case, soliciting the emotional responses of the orchestra members, especially those invested with many years together, might draw out a richer, fuller description of events in light of needing a new musical director.

It is also important to know where you as leader stand in the dilemma. Do you have vested interests in retaining what currently exists? Or do you support changing to another way or form? What do you stand to gain or lose with a particular resolution of the problem? Could your own values, beliefs, and opinions impede a fuller understanding of the situation? Do your current habits of mind influence or taint your reflections? For example, if you tend to value one person's views over others', do that person's ideas overshadow others' views in this situation?

The action associated with the description phase is to ensure that each person involved has ample opportunity to comprehend varied points of view as fully as possible. This is where personal, introspective reflection becomes outward sharing and action. The leader seeks to account for all viewpoints as part of comprehensively investigating the problem. He or she might set up and facilitate processes that ensure participation by everyone, not only the dominant or influential few. It also means hearing from those who might be skeptical of changes or opposed to new developments. As Dewey pointed out, just because a certain viewpoint has become predominant does not mean that other viewpoints have necessarily disappeared. They may remain under the surface, reemerging at the first available opportunity.

Key Questions in Description

1. Who is involved? What is their role, responsibility, or interest in the matter? What group(s) might they represent?
2. What occurred and what were the consequences? What issues— for instance, academic, financial, social, or political—are present?
3. What interests or viewpoints might be at odds? Are there multiple perspectives presented? If not, why not? Is there already consensus on the matter?
4. Between the different sides of the dilemma, what are your initial leanings? Why? If you do not have a particular leaning in the situation, what accounts for that?
5. What are your empathies and sympathies as a leader? What leadership "blind spots" do these suggest to you?

I = INTERPRETATION

The second phase of the method is analytical and interpretive. It harnesses ethical language to assist in exploring the dilemma. The leader attempts to identify the actual ethical tensions involved and name them. Consider whether the situation is based on mutually exclusive beliefs among participants or groups. Are there universal duties or desires at issue? For example, if one side feels that school rules must be upheld no matter the circumstances while the other side considers rules to be guidelines, not precepts, then an ethical tension exists between how rules should be interpreted. If the case involves advocates for a solution that seems to meet the the majority's needs over maintaining a specific virtue, then tensions occur between utilitarian and virtue-oriented individuals. By identifying the conflict and tensions using ethical language, the leader can lessen the emotions involved while continuing to understand and analyze the situation.

Take, for example, the dispute that arose in a school that was seeking funding for smaller class sizes. The state government had defined a criterion related to poverty status in the student body that schools were required to meet in order to receive funds. The principal of one school found that if she figured her absentees one way, then her school would qualify under state formulas, resulting in class size reductions of eight students per classroom. However, her method, while legal, did not quite follow the letter of the law in meeting the specific requirements for the new funds. Her dilemma was whether to use such a formula to calculate student poverty toward the good end of smaller class sizes, or to use the traditional formulas found in the rules governing funds—utility versus duty.

This example illustrates how Dewey's identification of different ethical tensions can be helpful. Is this a problem of social order where hierarchy and authority are involved? Is it a problem of change conflicts in which new forms or ways are challenging more traditional ones? Are these old and new ways mutually exclusive? To what extent is this a problem of private versus public interests? Who is most vested in each side of the argument? All of these questions can clarify the meaning of the different arguments going on within the ethical dilemma. Using Dewey's dilemma identification—class and mass, old and new, private and public—the leader can seek further analytical intepretation to understand what is occurring.

Interpretation may seem overwhelming at first because of the complexity of an ethical dilemma. It may also appear to lead away from a straightforward resolution. Keep in mind that interpretation is not about reaching a singular agreement about solutions to the problem, but rather about identifying, exploring, and even debating the underlying tensions of the dilemma. We suggest that debating the merits of different ethical frames of understanding is a good idea because the process can clarify issues and arguments made by the different sides. It can also begin the process of discerning alternatives to the dilemma by inviting creativity and imagination in looking for viable next steps.

Key Questions in Interpretation

1. What are the ethical tensions represented by the problem? Is there tension between different universal beliefs held by members? Is it a question of what is virtuous for individual members versus what is virtuous for the group? Is it a question of utility versus duty?
2. Are there problems of association in the case related to social order, change conflicts, or private versus public interests?
3. Has there been ample opportunity to discuss and debate the different ethical frameworks? Are there additional issues or concerns that have surfaced as a result?
4. Do the tensions imply possible actions by the leader or the group? If so, then move on to the rehearsal phase.

R = REHEARSAL

Once interpretation of the ethical tensions has been accomplished, start thinking through possible courses of action and strategies to employ toward effecting change. Dewey and Fesmire refer to this stage as dramatic rehearsal because we do not act; rather, we reflect upon the possibilities that might happen if a certain course of action is adopted. As much as possible, we play out the consequences that might occur as well as posit some unintended outcomes. Through this rehearsal, we are in a better position to make a decision.

Rehearsal begins by hypothesizing the "what-ifs" of a situation before acting. We become more conscious of the possibilities, the true nature of the situation, and our own limitations in understanding the action that we might take. Having analyzed tensions, we are better able to predict what might happen as we attend to our wants and desires, as well as to the duties and responsibilities of our leadership. We take into account more of the complexity of satisfying competing ethics. For example, as a principal, you might want the new hands-on science curriculum offered by the district. But in assessing the costs of implementing the curriculum, you realize that the development money needed to train faculty might be in direct conflict with your duty to balance the school budget and manage resources. Your wants and desires may not line up with your need to be a fiscal manager of resources. Duties and desires can be, at the least, evaluated in this rehearsal phase of deliberation.

We can also predict consequences based upon Dewey's problems of association by looking at social order, change conflicts, and private-public interests. For example, when the SPCO board became aware of the financial situation for the chamber orchestra, they might have considered the implications of social ordering. Suppose the players were designated according to a hierarchy, with some identified as key members who were essential to the orchestra, and others considered expendable players who might be replaceable. A possible action would be that the SPCO would retain only key players, release expendable ones, and hire extras as needed at a much lower rate. If, however, the SPCO's social ordering was egalitarian and all musicians were expected to be treated in the same way regardless of status, seniority, and specialty, then a possible solution might be to release all players. The result would be that the SPCO would no longer be a viable ensemble.

The action in the rehearsal phase moves beyond imagining possibilities to proposing actual courses of action. This can lead to a better understanding of the challenges associated with the dilemma. In the SPCO case, the board eventually rejected the placement of musicians in a hierarchy because it would have compromised one of the most important things about chamber orchestras—the development of a tight ensemble sound that comes from a small group playing together over a period of time. Considering the possible consequences of an action prepares for the next phase of working an ethical dilemma. For the SPCO, this might involve determining the costs and benefits needed to retain the ensemble, calculating the demands on the group, considering the upset with player changes, and projecting the public's response to the orchestra's actions.

Key Questions in Rehearsal

1. What are possible actions and the consequences of those actions in the dilemma?
2. What might be intended and unintended consequences of your actions and the actions of others? How might others respond to the possible actions you could take?
3. To what extent have you fully explored possible actions and their outcomes? Are some actions idealized? What might be reasonable or likely? What might be impossible to execute? Dramatic rehearsal might help answer these questions.
4. Once you have fully explored the possibilities, what possibilities have become clearer for you? For the group? How do you imagine yourself and the group executing them?

R = REDISCERNMENT

The process of rediscernment involves discovering new energy for the challenge at hand through heightened understanding of the complexity, tension, consequences, and likely possibilities of any given action. It can break us out of the language that we typically use to frame our approaches. It can encourage new ways to think about the problem and its resolution. Language tools like simile and metaphor may be applied to reframe the dilemma based upon the description and analysis already done. For example, using the metaphor of SPCO as family promotes a different set of options than considering it to be a for-profit organization. Other creative techniques like employing visualization and mind mapping can generate alternatives that might be original in meeting the needs of all involved. Thus, rediscernment has an a priori quality of new understandings to it.

An acknowledgment of all points of view as part of rediscernment is important. This way, as new possibilities are articulated, the current context is honored. If the new possibility is not actually new but rather a reworking of an existing plan or strategy, then the context helps to identify why this might be the best choice.

Rediscernment requires that the next iteration of working the dilemma include a more coherent description of the problems that precipitated the dilemma in the first place. Progress in working the dilemma can come through its redefinition or redescription. For example, a person may experience racism in the workplace and be faced with how to deal with it. The dilemma could be whether to confront the individuals involved and risk further ostracism or to put up with the treatment without any overt action. While the situation may appear to be a very personal attack, the person might learn in gathering background information that the problem is not personal but exists for others as well. Changing the discernment of the problem from "my personal problem with racist actions" to a collective social concern with racism in the workplace shifts the entire approach to the dilemma. It also expands the scope of who might be involved and who might be affected.

Rediscernment calls for action that harmonizes interests and needs, assesses consequences, indicates new actions for the group, and seeks to emerge from the rhythm and harmony of the process so that there is a sense of grace that overlays the actions to be taken. We may not associate grace with the workings of a major organizational dilemma or use terms such as *harmony* and *rhythm*, but there is a rhythm to conflict where its very pulse waxes and wanes as new things develop. Harmony can come, even in agreeing to disagree. And we want to be careful that rediscernment is not confused with consensus or compromise.

While consensus refers to the group's willingness to let a specific action move forward, the rediscernment phase is more about reaching a better understanding of the situation before any action is taken. Compromise is generally thought of as finding the middle ground where people can agree, losing and winning something in the process. Differing from that, rediscernment seeks to build action out of a revised picture of the dilemma. There may be elements of both compromise and consensus in this process, but ultimately the goal is a better understanding of the situation to allow resolution and enable action to be taken. Only then can the group become more facile and effective.

In part, the SPCO's financial problem was interwoven with the need for a new music director, the cost of whom was a significant percentage of the SPCO's budget. However, when the players agreed to a pay cut, they helped the board rediscern the problem and think differently about the directorship. Rather than retain the new conductor, the board chose to redefine the music director position as a revolving one, held by five highly respected musical consultants like violinist Joshua Bell and musician Bobby McFerrin. Based on their strengths and focus areas, each musician would "consult" with the orchestra on programming and performance. The board saw this as an opportunity to develop the capacity of the SPCO while appealing to a broader audience than one music director might be able to accomplish. And they could do so within the constraints of the orchestra's current budget. For now, the solution appears to be working, and the SPCO has developed a way of collectively working through problems that will likely increase its capacity to handle future challenges.

Finally, rediscernment may promote different organizational responses. A chamber orchestra used to having one music director will need to develop new ways to work with its five pro tem consultants serving in the one position. In addition, communication of the new habits is enhanced by a clear description of what brought the group to the place where change became necessary in the first place. This means that the original dilemma, the process for working through it, and the new directions must be clearly communicated. This helps to work through the second-guessing that might take place and offers a new cultural interpretation for the group to work with.

Key Questions in Rediscernment

1. What new understanding do you have of the dilemma? To what extent does it address the interests of all concerned?
2. Are there different organizational and personal habits that might be required as you move forward with resolution of the dilemma? Would certain habits or routines need to be modified or eliminated to satisfactorily work out of the situation?

3. Is the original story of the dilemma coherently communicated in the plan to address it? What do you need to reclarify the problem?
4. To what extent are everyone's needs and interests accounted for so that there is at least tacit harmony in the organization?
5. Are there metaphors that might help to describe yours or others' understanding of the situation? If so, what are these?

TOWARD RESOLUTION

Often the resolution of a dilemma appears to be correct, but this seeming correctness is based more upon the facts as we would like them to appear than as they actually are. This means that we need to approach dilemmas with an attitude of openness, especially in considering our own assumptions and blind spots. Pragmatists recognize that applying certain principles such as utilitarianism or virtue-ethics to a dilemma can be seductive because it can underscore our own views of the situation. Moreover, as we wrestle with ethical dilemmas, it might be easier to draw upon past practice than attempt to engage in discernment and reflective action.

The method that we advocate allows us to be conscious of conflicting data as they exist in all their complexity. If we are not mindful of the specific contexts, conflicts, and tensions as presented uniquely in specific situations, then we may arrive at a course of action that has nothing to do with the problem at hand.

Those with some background in organizational theory may recognize that people often rely upon familiar and tested strategies and actions regardless of the problem or dilemma. According to folk wisdom, it is the adage "To the hammer, everything looks like a nail." So breaking through to a new problem-solving method is definitely a challenge, but that is exactly the point of using this method. As we stated before, if there is no real growth in the organization among the individual participants or groups involved, then there is no chance of improvement and progress. This does not mean that previously held ideas should be summarily done away with. Rather, in holding them to the same standard of examination that new information is generally subject to, leaders have a better chance to work the problems in a meaningful way.

SUMMARY

Informed by the work of Dewey and Fesmire, our inquiry method for ethical deliberation seeks to be useful and pragmatic for school leaders. The criteria to determine its utility are that it is exploratory, dynamic, imaginative, and capacity building. The SPCO's dilemma illustrates how the processes of discernment and action work together in the four phases of the method—description, interpretation, rehearsal, and rediscernment, which together form the acronym *DIRR*. While appearing to be serial, the method progresses from description to rediscernment and cycles back as new information or insight occurs.

We hope that this method provides you with a systematic approach to resolving ethical dilemmas and achieving workable solutions. As a leader, you should not feel compromised or that you have given away too much. You have considered all parties and their perspectives as much as possible. You have tried to be open, creative, and discerning. While one solution might not necessarily be ideal and some might disagree with the course of action taken, you can remain open to reflection and reconsideration. By considering the DIRR method, we hope you are better prepared to act progressively in ways that are mutually beneficial to individuals as well as to the organization as a whole.

Part III

APPLICATIONS

CHAPTER 7

Cases to Consider

Educational leaders often regard their ethical decisions in practical terms. Prudently, they investigate the details of the situation along with determining the appropriate action to be taken. They consider antecedent factors like who's involved; what are key concerns, issues, and experiences; and what occurred. They also weigh consequences relating to the outcomes desired, who might be affected, and who benefits or loses from the actions. There might be state and federal regulations that stipulate certain requirements for school funding, for reporting test scores, and for how schools must approach children with exceptional needs. Leaders may need to examine very firmly held personal or professional values, perhaps in direct conflict with others to whom they are accountable. These make for ethical dilemmas in deciding what to do.

In this chapter, we present seven cases that illustrate various kinds of conflicts that demand ethical decision making. Each case is briefly described and then presented in greater detail. As the reader, you may wish to read through all of the cases or selectively choose ones that are of more interest or relevance to you. As the DIRR method is applied, we offer some discussion questions related to each of the four components in the cycle—description, interpretation, rehearsal, and rediscernment. We also suggest some specific questions related to each case. These questions may serve you as you work these ethical dilemmas and consider what actions might be appropriate.

Begin by considering the extent to which the information provided is adequate. Do you as a reader know who the key players are in the case? Is the primary decision maker different from the administrator in

charge? Are there contextual factors related to the specific school or lo-
cale that might be relevant to resolving the case? For example, in a student truancy case, the location of the school and its multiethnic student
body factored into how students were treated differently. This kind of
background information may be necessary to consider. Another case involving a similar attendance problem but situated in a different school
might generate a different set of issues or concerns.

What are the legal, ethical, and moral issues in the case? Discrimi-
nating between actions that are deemed legal and illegal is different
from deciding what might be a good thing to do or the right action to
take. In a case about employee conduct, the key decision maker was
the supervisor who was determining whether to reprimand the employee for inappropriate conduct. Some key issues in that case involved due process in handling personnel matters, treating all employees fairly, and determining appropriate conduct in an educational
setting. If the decision maker were a fellow employee rather than the
supervisor, the dilemma might involve a different set of issues, like
speaking truthfully about the situation or remaining loyal to the colleague. Rather than due process and fair treatment, the case might be
more personal in nature and involve considering what individual values are most pressing.

It is also useful to consider whether more information would be helpful in the case. Perhaps information about certain school policies or
laws is needed to clarify regulations and legal aspects of the case. Has
this situation ever occurred in the school district? What has been the
policy in the past? Are there legal rules that bind what action should be
taken? Might a specialist or legal consultant be able to assist? Should
further investigation occur before action is taken?

Consider whether other individuals factor in as key decision makers.
For example, in a case involving a teacher, principal, and superintendent, the decision varies if placed in the hands of the school principal or
the top system-level administrator. Reconsidering who is responsible
broadens the perspectives considered as well as the consequences for
people involved in the case. There are additional concerns if we must
think about implications for administration beyond the classroom, or
even beyond the school building. Suppose the governing body is the
school board. How might ethical deliberation be considered if it must

be negotiated among various members of a diverse school board? What is the relationship between the school superintendent and the school board?

If other key actors are involved in the case, try to account for their perspectives. Japanese filmmaker Akira Kurosawa depicted three versions of an incident in the film *Rashomon*, stringing one version after the other and allowing the viewers to conclude who was indeed telling the truth. Changing one's perspective is a useful means for balancing the perspective of the primary decision maker with others who might play key roles in the situation. This strategy takes the primary decision maker out of the drama, allowing some distance and perhaps objectivity. It can illumine alternatives, which might not have been available initially.

The specific questions listed in table 7.1 may be useful as you engage in working the ethical dilemmas. These questions align with the DIRR method and probe conflicts that might underlie the situation at hand.

CASE 1: CHOOSING A NEW PRINCIPAL

Synopsis. To fill an opening for a principalship at Pacific Heights Elementary School, the superintendent has appointed a five-member committee to conduct a search and interview candidates. Of the three candidates interviewed, the first choice of the committee is not the superintendent's choice. Her preferred candidate was ranked third by the committee. With no time to conduct another search, what should the superintendent do?

Detailed Narrative. For Superintendent Kate Feinstein, choosing a new principal for Pacific Heights School will not be easy. The individual appointed must turn around a chronically underperforming school with low student achievement, poor attendance, and high teacher turnover. The problems have been so long standing that the most recent principal lasted only six months. Because the school failed to meet benchmarks for the past three years, it will be restructured and heavily monitored. Whoever is selected to be principal must take on the problems while Feinstein closely supervises the reform process.

Table 7.1. DIRR Questions

DIRR Method	Key Elements	Questions
D=Description	Problem	What appears to be the problem that needs resolution?
	Key persons	Who is involved? What are their roles, responsibilities, or interest in the matter?
	Sequence of events	What occurred and when?
	Issues, concerns	What issues and concerns—social, political, economic, or academic—are present in the case?
	Interests represented	Are there individual or group interests in this situation? Do certain individuals represent specific groups?
I=Interpretation		*Sources of ethical tension*
	Duties-based	What is the right action based on rules or duties? To what extent do the leader's duties bind her/him to a specific course of action?
	Desires-based	What is in the best interest of the majority? What are utilitarian concerns?
	Virtue ethics	What constitutes good leadership? To what extent does one's personal and professional life contribute to making an ethical decision?
	Group or societal ethics	What constitutes "good" for the group or society?
	Social order conflicts	Does social order (e.g., who responds to whom, who is related to whom) need to be considered in resolving this case? Is there a hierarchical relationship (e.g., employee to supervisor) or dominant group involved in the case?
	Old versus new	Are there traditional views or customs that are being challenged by new or different ones?
	Private versus public	How do private interests clash with public concerns? Is this a private matter or does it involve public interests?
R=Rehearsal	Consequences	What might be some possible actions and likely consequences? Are there unintended consequences that might occur?
	Timetable	What are some short-term outcomes or long-term outcomes from the actions to be taken?
R=Rediscernment	Reframing	What language tools (e.g., simile, metaphor) or creative techniques (e.g., visualization, mind mapping) could be used in reframing the problem?
	Inclusiveness	As much as possible, have all viewpoints been included and given due consideration in resolving the situation?
	Reassessment	Have new information and insight helped redefine the problem? Is there a revision of the dilemma?

The position vacancy was announced, and a five-member search committee was constituted with two principals, a teacher, a curriculum resources person, and a parent. The committee was directed to review applications, interview the top candidates, and make its recommendations to Superintendent Feinstein. With an applicant pool of only three candidates, the committee chose to interview all three.

The first candidate, Allison Steiner, was curriculum coordinator at a nearby high school. With an impressive background in curriculum and instruction, she seemed to know the latest research and assessment strategies. Despite having only secondary school experiences, she might bring the academic rigor necessary if test scores were to improve. However, in the course of the interview, her communication and interpersonal skills appeared to be lacking; she came off sounding like a know-it-all. According to the curriculum resource person serving on the search committee, "Ms. Steiner's very competent in her area, but that's secondary school curriculum, not elementary. I wonder if she can handle the lower grades." It was also reported that while in her current position, Allison had created unrest among the faculty with a union grievance filed against her. A teacher on the committee had heard about this incident. But was it merely gossip?

Second to be interviewed was John Jacobs, a second-grade teacher new to the district and just finishing his principal licensure program. Although well meaning, he did not have the requisite skills and experience as evidenced by his application and the vague responses given during the interview. It seemed unlikely that he could lead an underperforming school. The committee felt that John had potential and might make a good principal some day, but not right now and not at Pacific Heights.

The third candidate was Mary Jo McCarthy, a personable special education teacher who had taught for years in another elementary school. Like a doting grandmother, Mrs. McCarthy charmed the committee with her manner. Even though she was being interviewed, she passed around cookies and tea as if in her own home. She definitely had a calming effect, important if she was to work with an admittedly tough faculty. But could she lead the school in reform? Her knowledge of curriculum was limited. She didn't understand how to read data about student achievement and yearly progress. One principal on the search committee expressed these reservations. "It's likely Mary Jo will retire soon. Should we risk Pacific Heights on someone who will be out shortly? But maybe the school needs someone for the short term to heal the wounds amongst the faculty. Mrs. McCarthy could do that."

While the committee members were aware that they were only offering a recommendation to the superintendent, they became seriously invested in advocating for Mrs. McCarthy. All felt that she could learn what she lacked; moreover, her interpersonal skills would go a long way toward healing the toxic school environment. Neither of the other two candidates was deemed adequate to the task, John because he lacked sufficient experience, and Allison because she lacked elementary school background as well as interpersonal skills.

Superintendent Kate Feinstein had doubts, wondering about Mrs. McCarthy's qualifications and motivation. If Mary Jo had been interested in gaining curriculum knowledge, she would have done so by now. And yes, she was close to retirement age. Would this administrative appointment mean a significant boost to her salary? Regardless of the motivation, could she work with Mary Jo on curriculum matters? Allison Steiner seemed the most knowledgeable in curriculum and assessment to lead Pacific Heights out of its restructured status. But the committee raised important concerns about her communication skills. Having gotten to know Allison through the synagogue where they attended, would choosing Allison be a biased choice? What about the second candidate, John Jacobs? Was he a viable alternative? With school scheduled to start in ten days and no time for conducting another search, Feinstein needed to appoint a principal for Pacific Heights as soon as possible. What should she do?

ADDITIONAL QUESTIONS TO CONSIDER

1. Good selection: Selecting the right person for a leadership role is important. How do you make a good selection? How important are the candidate's background knowledge, skills, and experience? What about personal relationships and communication skills?

2. Individual versus group: Is the superintendent obligated to the committee, or vice versa? What might be the immediate as well as long-term consequences from this decision?
3. Utilitarianism: From a utilitarian argument, how can the superintendent maximize the good for the school and for the district in choosing a new principal?
4. Compromise candidate: Is there a way to appoint someone whom both the committee and the superintendent might agree upon? Would that make John Jacobs a viable choice even if he lacks experience?
5. Sources of information: To what extent should the superintendent rely on prior information like knowing the individual outside of the professional setting? How does one determine the usefulness of information that might be hearsay or gossip?

CASE 2: PE EXEMPTION

Synopsis. The school district requires that all students in high school take a PE course, requiring students to suit up appropriately to participate. At Albertson High, a number of Arab American girls who wear veils as part of their Islam faith object to having to change, remove their veils, wear shorts, and play intramural sports with boys. The vocal Arab American community supports its daughters' boycott of PE classes. When the principal appeals for an exemption for her students, her boss, the school superintendent, objects.

Detailed Narrative. The school district requires that all students in high school take a PE course, demanding physical exertion and strenuous activity such as running, ball tossing, and water aerobics. Usually taken during the freshman year, the course requires that all students suit up appropriately to participate. This is a graduation requirement that applies uniformly to all three high schools in the district.

Of the three schools, Albertson High has a substantial number of students of Arabic decent, some who have lived in the United States for several generations and have assimilated into American culture. There were also those more recently emigrated from Syria, Lebanon, Yemen, Iran, and Iraq. Over the past decade, a more vocal Arab American community has evolved, uniting particularly those of more conservative Muslim backgrounds. In part, this was due to the increased attention and negative publicity against Arabic speakers and particularly Muslims. The Arab American community united to support its members in acculturating to a new country as well as in fighting off negative stereotypes directed against Muslims.

At Albertson, 60% of the student body are of Arabic descent, and of the Muslim girls, a number choose to wear the veil as part of their regular school dress. This had not been a problem until recently when some girls elected to sit out of PE class because of the dress requirement. At first, it was not clear why the girls were opting out of PE. But when it was learned that they objected to having to remove their veils, changing into shorts, and playing intramural games with boys, there seemed to be a general boycott of all PE classes with nearly 100 girls absent.

The athletic director in charge of all PE, health, and guidance classes raised the issue with the principal. She in turn spoke first to the Arab American counselor to get some insight into the situation. He recommended that she speak to a representative from the Arab American community, the director in charge of the local community center. It was clear from the community perspective that there was strong objection to having these Arab American daughters remove their veils and wear shorts. The community representative suggested that the principal appeal to the school district for an exemption from the graduation requirement. Together they decided that this might be the best course of action given the community feeling and the number of girls who had already boycotted classes.

The principal drafted a letter to the school superintendent making the request for the PE exemption. Her aim was to best serve the needs of the students at Albertson High, particularly the Arab American girls by accommodating their religious dress. She also asked the community representative to write a letter of support and present the community's views. He reiterated the importance of the tradition of wearing the veil for young Muslim women and asked that the school district honor the Arab American community's request.

However, the school superintendent was not easily swayed by the arguments made. From his viewpoint, all schools needed to maintain the same high standards and graduation requirements. One could not allow exemption for one group, especially those religious fanatics who chose to wear their religion so openly. This was a public school, after all, one of three high schools in the district, and he was bent on making sure that a standards-based education was maintained in all schools consistently. He also objected to the favoritism shown toward a more vocal Arab American community. "Just because they're a squeaky wheel doesn't mean they'll get greased!"

Such an exemption would need the approval of the school board. The members generally went along with the superintendent's wishes. In this case, it was clear that he would not be approving a PE exemption. Does the principal have any alternatives?

ADDITIONAL QUESTIONS TO CONSIDER

1. Leadership: Who needs to take action in this matter? Does the principal need to press the matter with the school superintendent and risk losing her job?
2. Consequences: What about the Arab American girls who have boycotted their PE classes? What will happen to them? Does this mean they will not graduate from Albertson?
3. Values in conflict: Are there specific values in conflict for the various groups in this case—the Arab American girls, their families, the Muslim community, the principal, the school superintendent, and the school board?
4. Religious freedom: To what extent must there be tolerance and religious freedom extended in this situation? Who is authorized to make that determination?
5. Equal educational opportunity: Is there an issue of equal educational opportunity in this case? If so, what provisions are being made to ensure that there is equal opportunity?

CASE 3: SEXUAL ENCOUNTER

Synopsis. A charming and charismatic department chair is rumored to have had numerous affairs with faculty members at school. However, that has not reflected in his performance on the job, and the principal has tended to ignore what were deemed "personal matters." Recently, the principal hired a 25-year-old science teacher who is attractive and somewhat naive. The department chair is making advances that border on being inappropriate and out of line. Should the principal step in?

Detailed Narrative. Tad McCutcheon had been at Heritage High for nearly fifteen years, serving for the past decade as the Science Department chair. During that time, his charismatic leadership had made people take notice of what was occurring there. Over the years, student achievement in science had shot through the roof. Science fair awardees were numerous; special recognition was given to competitive placements in the robotics and engineering competitions at the state level. Students were recognized for their projects in the National Youth Science Camp. The school even had two winning entries in the International Science and Engineering Competition held last year. No question, this department chair was responsible for these accomplishments. He was definitely a mover. Not only did his own students excel, but anyone taking a science course had done better than most schools in the district. McCutcheon was more than just a good teacher; he was a visionary leader who could move his department ahead of the pack.

Tad was also tall, dark, and very handsome with a classical Mediterranean profile. He seemed to be a natural-born athlete, very energetic, and competitive in tennis and golf. At 40, he was still single and was thought to be a very eligible bachelor. Women teachers at Heritage not only found him charming, but it was rumored that he had had numerous affairs with several faculty members.

These rumors had not troubled Principal Norman Santos in the past. He had hired Tad and had seen how the young man matured from a "kid wet behind the ears" to a competent and charismatic leader of the Science Department and also of Heritage High. There was no question that he was excellent. Was it Tad's fault that he was also good looking and that he attracted women like flies? Norman chose to let consenting adults do what they did as long as it didn't interfere with school morale and student achievement. His view was that this was a personal matter and that there should be freedom of choice.

But the current situation seemed different. Mr. Santos had recently hired a new teacher for the Science Department, Leah Plushenko, a 25-

year-old who had been a biologist doing research for several years before returning for teacher certification. A Russian by birth, she and her
family had immigrated to the United States when she was just 15.
While she seemed to be Western in most ways, there appeared to be an
"old country" way about her. At times, she seemed younger than her
years and more naive than most in handling students. Blond and petite,
she seemed so tiny compared to the juniors and seniors in her classes.

Tad McCutcheon, as Science Department chair, was her immediate
supervisor. He liked Leah from the start and was willing to go the extra
mile to make sure that she succeeded as a science teacher. They seemed
to get along well, and his help appeared to ease her transition into teaching at Heritage High. Tad would often stop by during recess or after
school to talk about lessons and how her teaching was going. When
asked about her progress, he reported that she was doing just fine.

One night after a parent-teacher meeting, Mr. Santos noticed lights
still on in Ms. Plushenko's biology lab. It was about 9:30 p.m., and that
seemed pretty late. Passing by the classroom, he noticed two silhou-
ettes huddled close together. "None of my business," he muttered under his breath.

The next afternoon at the faculty meeting, Mr. Santos had faculty
members working in smaller breakout groups by their respective departments. Walking around the room, he noticed that Tad was leading
the discussion in the Science Department group. Seated next to him
was a red-faced Leah Plushenko, who seemed uncomfortable and
somewhat fidgety. As Norman Santos walked by the group, he noticed
that Tad had his hand on Leah's thigh while he was talking. The others
in the Science Department didn't seem to notice. "Is this my business?"
Santos wondered. But Leah sure did look young. After all, she was the
same age as Norman's own daughter.

ADDITIONAL QUESTIONS TO CONSIDER

1. Rules, regulations, and guidelines. How would you as administrator determine if there was a sexual encounter in this case? What
   rules and regulations currently exist in your school organization to
   offer guidance? Once determined, are you obligated to act?

2. Determining faculty conduct: What determines good conduct on the part of faculty? How does this apply to those with supervisory responsibilities like department chairpersons and administrators?
3. Social order conflicts: To what extent does the hierarchical relationship between the teacher and her department chair need to be taken into account? Is it relevant to deciding what to do?
4. Private versus public considerations: Is this a private affair or does the case have consequences for the school community as a whole? What might be some unintended consequences in this case?

CASE 4: HOMECOMING

Synopsis. Homecoming at Tranquil Bay High, the state's oldest high school, is full of tradition and specific rituals that involve the practice of hazing sophomore classmates. This case illustrates the dilemma of an administrative intern attempting to retain specific cultural activities associated with the celebration while curbing the violence that has been escalating against students.

Detailed Narrative. Homecoming at Tranquil Bay High School follows the tradition of most high schools in the United States. Alumni of the school are invited to attend functions and reacquaint themselves with their community. It is also a time during school for friendly competition among the sophomores, juniors, and seniors to build school identity and a sense of belonging. At halftime during a football game with a school rival, the king and queen of homecoming are crowned along with a court of princes and princesses. After the game, the students attend a dance or other social to build school spirit.

However, Tranquil Bay homecoming activities in recent years have included hazing of the youngest class—the sophomores. While the practice of hazing is illegal in the state, it appeared to be getting more malicious at Tranquil Bay. Last year, on the Thursday night of homecoming week, juniors and seniors went on an all-night rampage of vandalism, writing obscene messages on teachers' cars and homes. Several sophomores were apparently "kidnapped" and duct-taped to stop signs in the community. Other captured boys were publicly humiliated by being forced to participate in public nudity or other demeaning activities. Several girls who were kidnapped reported being sexually and physically harassed. School administrators were inundated with calls from parents the day after the rampage.

Tranquil Bay's administrators tried a number of solutions to deal with the homecoming hazing. A few years ago, many of the unofficial activities were traced to a group of about fifty senior male and female athletes known as the Senior Sports Club. A very cliquish and exclusive group, the club was suspected of being responsible for much of the clandestine hazing, including the Thursday-night rampage. The administration decided that it would dismantle the Senior Sports Club and create a more inclusive group called the Student Spirit Club, which would be open to all students. But some senior boys formed what they nicknamed the "Senior Pimp Club," wearing sweatshirts announcing their club with the slogan "Come Ride My Pony," supposedly referring to the school's mascot. Several fights broke out during homecoming week, resulting in a Thursday rampage that was worse than ever. The administration decided to refer all complaints to the police and "just let the community handle it." This was also an unmitigated disaster, as an editorial in the local paper wondered, "What do we pay administrators for?"

The following year, the administration considered canceling homecoming altogether, but because community outcry was so great, it recanted. While those who were negatively affected by the hazing were clamoring for changes in homecoming week, many vested in the old traditions, as well as the community at large, placed a great deal of pressure on the administration to continue all the traditions and activities. So the administrators had an ethical dilemma on their hands.

The principal, Hal Spencer, decided to give the problem to a newly appointed administrative intern, Shelly Sakamoto. She had been an English teacher at Tranquil Bay and later department chair for a number of years. Her familiarity with the high school and community would be a plus. Hal realized that it was a tough assignment for a novice administrator, but at present he could not spare his other assistant principals for this thorny assignment.

When given the assignment, Shelly wondered why the different strategies initiated by administrators had not worked. For the most part, administrative interventions to control the hazing had been unilateral and top down. Teachers had not developed ownership of the solutions. They were not asked, nor had they volunteered any ideas toward a solution. The students were only consulted after the fact, and the community was not invited for input, either through informal means such as coffee hours to discuss the matter or through more formal contacts with the local police and city offices. Recommended solutions were based on information gleaned by the administration. When changes failed to curb the maliciousness, the administrators felt isolated and frustrated by the problem. Basically, they resigned themselves to a week that would be, in the principal's words, "just another one of life's trials." But an assistant principal said, "If this community doesn't wake up soon, some kid is going to get killed." In reflecting on the problem, Shelly realized that her own empathies in the situation were influenced by wanting to do a good job while not making the administrative team look bad for not having come to some meaningful solutions. As an administrative intern, did she even have the political clout to implement a solution while others with more experience had failed so miserably?

ADDITIONAL QUESTIONS TO CONSIDER

1. Duties and desires: What is the right action to take, and what good outcomes might be desirable?
2. Moral, ethical, and legal concerns: If hazing is illegal in the state, what are some legal issues or concerns to be considered? Should these be dealt with differently than ethical or moral issues? Why or why not?
3. Utilitarianism: What is best for the school as a whole, and who should determine that? Who needs to be involved in the deliberation?
4. Preserving traditions: Are there values that the school might want to retain and reinforce during this homecoming celebration? At what cost should traditions and customs be retained?
5. Authority: Does Shelly, the administrative intern, have sufficient authority to make a decision in this case? If not, what course of action might she take?

CASE 5: ACADEMIC FREEDOM

Synopsis. All faculty members have e-mail access in their school. Usually the administration sends out notices and information to everyone through the electronic mail server. It is generally thought that having e-mail access is the best way to communicate uniformly to the school community. This case illustrates how one e-mail fires up a barrage of comments when an individual teacher sent a message to her colleagues.

Detailed narrative. Soraya didn't realize how one little e-mail could create such a stir. Actually, when she first sent it out, there was hardly a ripple. It seemed an important statement for educators who were for peace. The e-mail had been from a colleague at another school and was being circulated by friends in the social justice network across the state. For those who might be interested, there was a contact person and suggestions for supporting the peace and social justice network. Soraya figured that those who were interested could write to the address, and those who were opposed could simply delete the e-mail. So she added a note of her personal endorsement and clicked on the Send button to forward the e-mail message to colleagues in the whole school.

A day later Soraya received one e-mail in support. Another day passed and another query. By day three, there was a message requesting that the listserv be used only for "school and work-related" e-mail messages. Next came the following e-mail:

> I find any kind of propagandizing on the Internet offensive, even if I agree with the propaganda. It's difficult enough to get through all the legitimate business e-mails without having to trash unwanted ones unrelated to my job. Delete my name if you continue to send this kind of e-mail!

At that point, the e-mail barrage began with those supporting the statement for peace and the use of the Internet to say so. The one lone voice of dissent kept firing back messages like a ping-pong ball.

> This has nothing to do with "free speech." The question is, Does someone have the right to tie up my e-mail account with matters unrelated to my job? I receive up to 40 e-mails a day, and sometimes it takes me three hours or more to read and respond to them. I don't mind e-mails related to school. But half of the e-mail is stuff that has nothing to do with

school! It wastes my time, time that is being paid for by the school. If Lincoln Middle is paying for my e-mail account, my use of the Internet at work should be limited to school business. No politics or foreign policy or religion or whatever the heck else one might personally think will "affect us all." By all means, engage in debate to your heart's content, but not over our school server. To do so is an inappropriate use of the e-mail account that Lincoln has provided us!

Then others began sending messages, some blasting the dissenting voice who remained in the shadows and anonymous. Other messages started targeting Soraya personally and questioning her leftist leanings. Even Soraya was beginning to wonder about her Lincoln Middle School colleagues with whom she had spent the past decade.

ADDITIONAL QUESTIONS TO CONSIDER

1. Academic freedom and free speech: To what extent is this case about academic freedom and free speech? What is the proper use of a school's listserv? For information only? For only approved communication? To omit politics, foreign policy, or religion amounts to censorship, doesn't it? But how much restriction on access should there be? Most schools do this to protect students. Do faculty also need that protection?
2. Decision maker: What is the administrator's responsibility? Can the administrator shut the listserv down and place sanctions against users? If so, what is the recourse to this action from those who have been silenced?
3. Communication: How does having e-mail communication challenge existing modes to connect and communicate with each other?
4. Acceptable behavior: What about net etiquette? What is acceptable e-mail behavior on a school's listserv, and who should be monitoring it?

CASE 6: LEADERSHIP AWARD

Synopsis. Reviewing applicants for a prestigious leadership award, Leon notices that one of the applicants is Randall Grey, a dynamic high school principal about whom he knows much more than the others. Leon's best friend is related to Randall and over the past months has been sharing information about Randall's personal life. Is this information even relevant when considering this leadership award?

Detailed Narrative. Notifications were sent out in early January to let candidates know that they had been selected for a prestigious community leadership award. There were seven principals who were selected for the final round. All seven were asked to submit applications answering questions about their school leadership, changes they had made and implemented, and their successes as well as the challenges they had overcome in their schools. In addition, the candidates were to submit testimonial letters from school personnel, parents, community members, and students in support of their leadership. Each nominee would be interviewed by a review panel of judges who would make the final selection. The winner was to receive a $15,000 cash award for his school and a $10,000 personal award for himself.

Representing his association of educators, Leon was pleased to be on the review panel. He knew several of his fellow panelists; one was a professor, another a retired superintendent, and the third a colleague from another school district. Leon wanted to support the efforts made by excellent school principals around the state. This would be a tremendous accolade for whoever was selected for this leadership award.

By mid-February, the coordinator contacted Leon and sent him a binder with the applications and information on ratings. The categories included leadership role, innovative program implementation, community involvement, challenges and changes made at the school, and plans for using the leadership award in furthering school improvement. It all seemed straightforward until Leon saw the applicant list.

Among the applicants who had made the final cut was Randall Grey, a principal of a rural high school. He had served as administrator for more than a decade at the same secondary school. In the capacity of principal, he had led for the past six years. A dynamic individual with much charisma and personality, Randall was building a collaborative learning community. He had involved numerous community groups in a literacy initiative linked with technology that seemed to be producing significant student achievement results. The record looked impressive, at least according to his application and the supporting letters.

The problem was that Leon had more information about Randall Grey's personal life. Randall was the brother-in-law of Ed Kowolski, Leon's best friend from college. Unfortunately, over the past several months, Ed had been sharing his concerns that Randall was becoming more of a tyrant at home. His aggressive behavior toward his wife, Ed's little sister, seemed to be bordering on spousal abuse. At least that was from Ed's description of the situation. But then Ed had never really liked his brother-in-law, so there might have been some hostility building over the dozen or so years that the couple had been married. But were these personal concerns to be raised by a reviewer for a leadership award? This was, after all, a confidential matter shared among friends. Yet with this personal history, Leon felt that he might not fairly judge Randall's capacity as a leader. Could he be unbiased as he interviewed Randall? Should he opt out as a reviewer? Was it already too late for that? he wondered. Perhaps he really should opt out of rating Randall because he had more information than the other reviewers did.

One of the applicants for the leadership award had mentioned being part of a cohort of principals trained by Professor Terri Brookfield, another member of the review panel. Would Terri also opt out from assessing that applicant? Certainly she would have more information about that applicant and possibly a biased view in favor since she had trained him. Leon wondered about the potential conflict of interest there. Should he raise that question as well? What would be the ethical thing to do?

ADDITIONAL QUESTIONS TO CONSIDER

1. Personal versus professional: How does Leon's personal relationship with the principal or his brother-in-law factor into being a good reviewer? Does this make for a moral-ethical dilemma for Leon?
2. Conflict of interest: What constitutes a "conflict of interest"? Does Leon's friendship with the principal's brother-in-law qualify? What about the conflict of interest for Professor Brookfield? Should Leon raise this as an issue to the review panel? Why or why not?

3. Leadership qualities: What constitutes good leadership? Should a principal's personal life as well as his professional work contribute to that?
4. Additional involvement: Who should be involved in resolving this situation? Who might be consulted for advice in this case? What additional information would be useful in deliberating further?
5. Private and confidential: Is some information personal and private? What should be kept confidential and not revealed?

CASE 7: CAREER INTERFERENCE

Synopsis. Having established a strong leadership team, Principal John Freire might lose his talented assistant principal, Janelle Wright. The superintendent has told him of a principalship opening next year, the third year of Janelle's contract. If John grants permission for her to break her contract, the superintendent has made clear that the job will be hers. What should Principal Freire do?

Detailed Narrative. As principal of Crispus Attucks High School, John Freire recruited an excellent leadership team to boost student achievement. Janelle Wright is the assistant principal in charge of instruction, and he negotiated a three-year contract for her at premium salary. Considered one of the most effective teacher trainers statewide, Janelle has helped teachers individualize their approach to language arts so that their teaching can become more precise and student centered. In her short time at Crispus Attucks, she has done the same for the faculty, and they love her.

In August, before the new school year was scheduled to open, Freire received an e-mail from the superintendent:

> John, I know the timing might not be the best, but Banneker Elementary is opening next year, and I need a good principal there. I was thinking Janelle could easily slide into the position and hit the ground running. She has the necessary administrative experience, and your faculty sings her praises. Of course, I wouldn't poach her if you say she should stay at Attucks since she's under contract. But I'd really like to post her at Banneker.

John had wanted to avoid this kind of situation when he negotiated three-year contract assignments with the district. In the past, the district had taken fairly new assistant principals and placed them in principalships to either sink or swim. Freire advocated for a longer training period to support leadership development and create stability in schools. Specifically, he negotiated three-year contracts for his two assistant principals to ensure that they remain at Attucks.

His first hire was Assistant Principal Don Potter who took over daily school monitoring and management. Don collected data on aspects such as lunch discipline, absenteeism, and parent contacts to predict where student support might be needed. His greatest strength was in number crunching and data management, not people skills. John frequently had to mediate between Potter and the office staff, but that was worthwhile given Don's systems analysis expertise.

Janelle Wright was Potter's opposite. Personable and genuinely likable, she knew teaching, she knew kids, and she knew what motivated teachers. Once hired at Attucks, she began conducting a series of teaching observations and meetings with faculty. By the end of the first term, Janelle had helped each teacher diagnose ways to differentiate instruction in the classroom. She even talked the most resistant veteran into trying a new teaching approach. She established a peer-review system that promoted teachers learning from each other through mentoring and coaching. Her work as instructional leader and faculty developer was beginning to show in terms of student achievement.

Last year, there was improvement in Attucks's test scores, but not enough to get the school off Annual Yearly Progress (AYP) status. This was Freire's most pressing concern. Over the summer, the leadership team had used Potter's systems analysis and Wright's teaching diagnoses to devise a comprehensive yet workable school improvement plan. Freire was excited to see how the school would fare this year, and so far, all signs were positive. Routines were in place, benchmarks were set, and teachers knew what was expected and had support to achieve the targets. With another year at least to work the plan, Attucks High should start taking off.

What about Janelle's future? She did want to become a principal some day and have a school that reflected her style of coaching and mentoring teachers. Freire could support that because she certainly was competent. She also was not young. She had spent many years in staff development, and this venture into administration was fairly new. John also knew that her husband had recently retired, so who knew how long she would want to remain in the school district?

Losing Janelle would set him back at least a year, maybe two. Attucks was a place that needed stability and commitment to ensure change. Losing a key member of the leadership team would be a severe blow to efforts at building relationships and implementing reform at the school. Now was not the time to do that. Anyway, by the time Janelle was free of her contract at Attucks, there would be other principal vacancies available, and she could easily get one of them.

On the other hand, who was he to block a talented person's career? John would be proud if she joined the principal ranks in the district. She probably should be told about the possibility at Banneker. Yes, he could train another person to step into the assistant principal position; after all he had done it before. Here was John's dilemma. What was good for Janelle seemed to be at odds with the school's needs, and what was good for the school seemed to get in the way of Janelle's career path. What should Freire do?

ADDITIONAL QUESTIONS TO CONSIDER

1. Decision maker: Whose decision is this? Is it right for the principal to interfere with Janelle's career? Is the principal obligated to follow the superintendent's request? Is it ethical for the superintendent to place John in this position?
2. One versus the many: Are the needs of the many (the students at Attucks School) more important in this case than the needs of the one (Assistant Principal Janelle Wright)?
3. Moral, ethical, and legal concerns: What are the moral, ethical, and legal considerations in breaking an employment contract?
4. Virtues: What values (e.g., truth, loyalty, responsibility, caring) might guide the principal's deliberation and decision making?
5. Old versus new clashes: To what extent is John seeking stability in his school while opposing change in leadership?

SUMMARY

In this chapter, seven cases were presented for the reader's consideration. Each case included a synopsis, a detailed narrative, and some discussion questions. While some of the cases were event specific, all suggested a historical context that encouraged the reader to dig deeper and
probe more rigorously. Unlike case narratives that present problems
and offer solutions, the reader is invited to consider personal as well as
professional reactions and alternatives to the dilemmas. Our experience
is that dilemmas do not simply get resolved; rather, they require working through in an iterative process that can evolve as one's knowledge
and skills increase.

CHAPTER 8

Teaching Ethical Deliberation

When we began this book project, our motivation was to write something for our students that would provide the necessary foundations and methods for grappling with the ethical dilemmas in their professional lives. We sought to provide sufficient background for understanding how ethical dilemmas emerge, how tensions might arise from different ways of reasoning, and how to negotiate among divergent viewpoints. Our assumptions were grounded in the need for democratic leadership that takes into account differences among individuals while at the same time seeking to emphasize the common goals and aspirations that draw us together as a society. We proposed an inquiry method that is based on democratic ethics and is applied as a metaethic to thinking through problems and situations.

In this concluding chapter,[1] we wrap up the journey by sharing how we have taught ethics and ethical deliberation. Coming from different backgrounds ourselves, we relate separate reflections on teaching in individual narratives. We then highlight similarities, differences, and challenges experienced in teaching. Beyond our own classrooms, we suggest that there are other venues where prospective and practicing school leaders engage in democratic practices. Whether in kindergarten or advanced placement physics, the classroom is a place to develop ethical thinking, citizenship, and leadership. As important as the classroom is the larger school community where discussion takes place among diverse groups of people, representing families, communities, businesses, and the society. We offer concluding thoughts about how teaching ethical deliberation applies to these classrooms and school communities.

TEACHING NARRATIVES

We teach at different institutions (one a private parochial institution, and one a public research-extensive university) in different geographic regions of the country (the midwestern region as compared with the Pacific west). As such, we decided to begin with separate narratives, describing each of our courses situated within our respective administrator preparation programs. Our individual narratives specify how we chose to teach about ethics and ethical deliberation. We note our similarities and differences across our university institutions as well as the challenges that we have encountered in teaching these courses over the years.

BRUCE KRAMER—
UNIVERSITY OF ST. THOMAS, MINNEAPOLIS

The University of St. Thomas, Minneapolis, is diocesan, Catholic, and urban. It is an exciting place to teach, partly due to the tensions that exist within our urban Minneapolis environment, and partly due to the cultural tensions within the university. Among these tensions are the cultural/historical tensions that come from starting out as a small men's liberal arts Catholic college, and the current reality of having professional schools in business, law, psychology, and education. And there are the inevitable tensions of having a Catholic mission while preparing students for the secular world of public school administration.

I teach two courses in ethics. The first, for principal licensure students, is entitled "Foundations of Educational Leadership: Ethical Perspectives." I have been teaching this course for ten years, more times than I wish to count. While not specifically required in the State of Minnesota Licensure Competencies, our institution requires ethics in order to earn the educational specialist degree that is closely aligned with licensure. In fact, we "bookend" our principal licensure program by beginning with a theoretical course in organizational theory and ending the program with the theoretical applications of ethics.

The course is organized around the central theme of judgment. Where there is judgment, there is choice, and where there is choice, there is an "ethical" decision. I assume that the dilemmas of leadership require using a variety of ways of thinking to reach fully informed decisions. I always try to help students become aware of their own particular sense of ethics. I also challenge them to examine their ethics for practicality, consistency, and efficacy. Student success is probably more dependent on their willingness to genuinely introspect and critically reflect than on any "one right way" of approaching the thorny issues that leadership and judgment raise.

Licensure students tend to see the licensure ethics course as relevant only after the fact. Rarely do I find a student who has ever before studied ethics in a philosophical way, and even rarer are students with an understanding of applied ethics beyond their own cultural inculcation. Students come into the course somewhat fearful; it has a reputation for requiring lots of reading. Nevertheless, as they analyze the exemplar dilemmas, I see them going through a process that begins with frustration and generally ends with a sense of knowledge about themselves and how they might participate as a leader in those very gray areas that define leader judgment.

An example of the type of activity that we do is to apply ethical analysis to the current accountability movement associated with No Child Left Behind. What does the course have to do with the lived experiences of students and current accountability movements? By the time we have covered the course syllabus, most students can analyze testing-based accountability models for what they are—a "scientific" attempt to superimpose a metaethical system upon their own professional work. Many students see current accountability movements, particularly as they play out in the testing realm, as examples of scientific reasoning gone awry. It is precisely for this analytical reason that I spend as much time as I do on defining ethical foundations. Without such definition, students are blissfully unaware that science is an ethical system in and of itself.

Just like the application of ethics to accountability, the application of ethics to any leadership situation is one of determining right ways and good ends. For me as instructor, this determination of "right" is best accomplished with serious attention to intertwining the philosophical foundations of ethics with specific applications to current leadership events as exemplars.

The second course that I teach is entitled "Leadership Ethics," a core course in our doctoral program. The focus of this course is to ensure that our doctoral students are able to see the moral language in their own leadership situations and to identify actions for themselves that are ethically compatible with their own beliefs and values. For the doctoral course, my work, together with my cofaculty member, is to seek the following good ends:

Students are to develop sharpened understanding of
- ethical history and philosophy
- the student's own moral leadership capacity
- areas of possible conflict between one's values and the values of others
- the consequences of conscious and unconscious ethical decisions by both the student and others

A heightened ability to
- analyze the ethical dimensions of a situation
- communicate an understanding of the ethical dimensions of any given dilemma
- seek ethical solutions to problems that look unsolvable
- imagine moral outcomes in situations for which moral solutions are not immediately discernible

A heightened appreciation for
- ethical inquiry
- the underlying ethical considerations of a personal/professional dilemma
- the ethical questions raised by privilege and difference
- the ethical questions raised by cultural traditions
- the shaping forces upon the student's own ethical beliefs
- the ethical connection and interdependence between desired self and the world that we desire

The students in the doctoral course represent a wide spectrum of professions—from the traditional K–12 educator to the business entrepreneur, with engineers, nonprofit managers, and police and fire safety persons thrown in for good measure. This spectrum enables rich discussions about the nature of ethics in different contexts and across professions. The leadership opportunities and challenges tend to unite students in their ethical deliberations, and this makes for broad learning opportunities.

Every time I teach either course, I agonize over readings and activities that will lead to meaningful outcomes in a course about how people make "right" decisions. In the doctoral course, we use a foundational ethics text for grounding the language and concepts, and we supplement this text with a variety of different genres of literature. For example, the Fasching and deChant (2001) text referred to in chapter 4 of this book, and the Fesmire (2003) text, *John Dewey and Moral Imagination*, critical to our method presented in chapter 6, are both used in the doctoral course. In the licensure course, I try to find a reading or two that will give some basic fundamental ideas about ethics, but we tend to read more in the literature specifically designed for educational leaders. I have been using Fullan's (2003) *The Moral Imperative of School Leadership* and Starratt's (2004) *Ethical Leadership*. I supplement these two texts with readings from Cornell West, bell hooks, and others critical of a majority style of ethical thinking, to challenge the students to see an ethical way of interpreting events that is extremely viable and helpful, particularly in the diverse contexts in which many of them will lead.

ERNESTINE ENOMOTO— UNIVERSITY OF HAWAII-MANOA, HONOLULU

For the past eight years, I have taught at the University of Hawaii-Manoa, a research-extensive university in the state of Hawaii. It is a flagship institution, serving statewide needs for undergraduate and graduate education in all disciplines. Our College of Education provides the majority of the teacher educators, counselors, and school administrators for the unified state system of education.

In our Educational Administration department, we offer a seminar in ethics as a special topics offering. As such, the same course number, EDEA780, may refer to a course on different topics such as curriculum issues, professional socialization, adult learning styles, as well as ethics. Currently there is no specifically designated course on the study of ethics in our program. The seminar is optional for those interested in the topic or with a need to fulfill the one-seminar requirement in their administrative preparation.

In the past, faculty members have taught ethics from a philosophical perspective and have emphasized historical and theoretical aspects of study, with limited connections made to any practical application of ethics. More recently, however, there has been a concerted effort to include ethical decision making as well as research on ethical dilemmas in educational practice. Building on this orientation, I developed my course as a graduate seminar emphasizing the importance of ethical decision making for effective educational leaders. In the course, I propose that school administrators need to know how to learn, adapt, and make on-the-spot decisions based on qualities of value and character. To do this, they must be able to reflect upon their own individual values and beliefs in education as well as their understanding of the community in which they live. My course is a journey of inquiry and exploration in the ways we think through ethical dilemmas and make decisions as school leaders.

The course begins by having students articulate their personal vision and values. They think through what they deem most important about education and their role as educators and leaders. They are also asked to construct a viable shared vision for the whole class. That is, everyone shares what they view as most important for our learning environment and determine what we want to value collectively. This shared vision becomes our framework for class discussions and participation throughout the term.

Using both the personal and shared vision statements, students examine various reality-based educational scenarios with issues such as conflict of interest, equal opportunity, confidentiality, and individual rights and responsibilities. Given an inquiry model like the DIRR method for ethical decision making, students are asked to determine whether the scenario poses an ethical dilemma, and if so, to consider how to apply at least three principles of ethical reasoning. For example, they might contrast the duty-based ethics with desires-based ethics, identifying the rationale and arguments for each case. They are also asked to consider what other ethical tensions factor into the decision making. Could personal virtues be called into question to make sound judgments? Do social order issues related to who is the boss confound decision making?

Students engage privately in writing about the cases as well as discussing them publicly in class. The cases provide simulated situations that are real and are often relevant to their personal experiences. Class discussions include time for students to present varying viewpoints. In some cases, we "try on each other's shoes" to examine alternative perspectives and consider consequences from diverse viewpoints. We might also argue from a position different from our personal preference to understand that point of view better. Students usually work through the logic and argument in small groups and then present their position to the class.

Throughout the term, students compile a portfolio of four different cases, with each write-up describing an ethical dilemma and providing supporting rationale, evidence gathered, and appropriate references. At least one case must be an original. As the teacher, I give feedback along the way and encourage students to revise their write-ups throughout the term. Often they choose to rewrite their first cases as their understanding and reasoning develop throughout the course. In addition to the case write-ups, students reflect upon the entire series of cases and prepare a summative statement about their entire portfolio. This overall reflection gives them a chance to identify ethical considerations in their individual administrative decision making and develop personal and professional guidelines for making such decisions.

After taking the course, students have commented on increasing their ability to problem solve, work through the ethical issues involved, and think through challenging questions that were relevant to their own lives. In the words of one student, the course "helped tremendously in developing and sharpening our decision-making capabilities." The students have valued having the opportunity to practice what is expected of them in terms of thoughtful deliberation and reflective action as educational leaders.

SIMILARITIES AND DIFFERENCES IN TEACHING APPROACHES

Reflecting upon our teaching, we asked ourselves, what is it that we seem to do in a similar fashion? First, we both strive to include diverse viewpoints through our selected readings and discussions. We offer contrasting and often critical perspectives in the readings for the course. Bruce particularly draws upon the critical theorists to probe what might be taken for granted. We also encourage varied perspectives through lively class discussions, debate, and dialogue.

A second similarity in our teaching is that we encourage our students to clarify their own codes of ethics. Bruce develops awareness by having his students examine their ethics for practicality, consistency, and efficacy. Ernestine has her students write out their personal codes and apply them in making decisions. We feel that this type of values clarification helps our students work through the process of translating their thinking into effective ethical actions as demonstrated in writing.

A third similarity is that, like Shapiro and Stefkovich (2005) and Strike, Haller, and Soltis (1998), we use case narratives in considering how to make ethical decisions. Examples of these are the cases in chapter 7. We also encourage students to write their own narratives and describe situations in ethical language. Demonstrating the DIRR method, we probe for description, interpretation, rehearsal, and rediscernment as students work the cases. We expect that students will demonstrate thoughtful introspection and critical reflection as they deliberate on what to do and what will result.

We also acknowledge some differences in our approaches to teaching. We teach in a different context that draws varied students. Teaching at a parochial institution, Bruce teaches both masters and doctoral students, primarily but not exclusively in education. By contrast, Ernestine teaches only masters students in educational administration in a public university setting. The age and experience of our students also influence our approach. In addition, there is a difference in the social diversity of our students. Ernestine teaches a fairly homogenous group of educators who have similar backgrounds. Bruce teaches a majority of educators, but there are also students from other professional backgrounds. Such differences lead to different styles of teaching in ensuring that a variety of perspectives are presented.

Our current styles of teaching, even though we each believe that diversity is important, are reflective of our perceptions of the needs of our students. For example, Ernestine sees her role as facilitating an ethical clarification process as her students engage in the exploration of "other" ideas. As most of her students share similar views on given ethical situations, she has them act out roles in small groups where they have to defend a viewpoint that they might not necessarily agree with. This dramatic enactment provides them with the opportunity to walk in another's shoes. Bruce engages his students by being more of a "provocateur." Because of a perceived regional way of seeing different situations as well as the natural reticence of many students, he tries to foster discussion by playing "devil's advocate."

As stated above, we try to support our students in clarifying their individual ethical codes. This is a point of convergence for us. We carry a strong value for individual students in our classrooms. We honor every student's slightly different approach and strive to allow for their individual differences as they explore their own personal beliefs. We agree that through the clarification of their belief systems, particularly as they compare their beliefs with their espoused sense of actions, they attain meaningful learning. However, we see some dilemmas around this issue that we discuss later.

Finally, we believe in supporting our students in translating their thinking into ethical action. This is probably the crux of the leadership context because we believe that school leaders need to act in ways that influence others. For example, in the school term, Bruce's students develop a cumulative case that requires many different modes of ethical thinking. They have commented that as a result, they don't look at situations in their personal or professional lives as simple and taken for granted. They are better able to work through the issues, concerns, and consequences that make the situation a messy dilemma.

CHALLENGES IN TEACHING

Our teaching challenges can be characterized in terms of the continuum of the contexts in which we teach. We agreed that where and whom we teach are important factors in helping us decide what actions we will take. From Ernestine's facilitation to Bruce's provocation, the actions we take are not prescribed but rather are based on individual diagnosis. We try to exercise the same ethical clarification, reflection, and discernment as our students in determining our own actions. At the same time, our actions are part of a continuum as well, within our respective departments, institutions, field of educational leadership, and current context of standards and accountability in American education.

The standards and accountability movement is a major factor in discussions about American education, whether we are in Hawaii or Minnesota. Ironically, at a time when we are more attentive to individual student needs, legislation directed toward accountability has taken a one-size-fits-all approach, holding everyone to the same academic standards, whether appropriate or not. We fear that accountability reform means that what is interpreted as ethical behavior for the school leader is increasingly prescribed by the dictates of standards-based education and other accountability factors. It is possible that standards lend themselves to "button-down" thinking about what is right versus what is wrong. This current context poses the same ethical dilemma in leadership preparation programs as in public education, namely how to honor individual differences while achieving academic standards directed toward the common good.

Despite concern over the external standards of the National Council for Accreditation of Teacher Education (NCATE), the Interstate School Leaders Licensure Consortium (ISLLC), and others, we remain optimistic. If in applying the standards there is the space for inquiry and critique, then it is also possible to encourage critical and original thinking where individuals are asked to reflect, discern, and reason through their actions. This is the kind of ethical deliberation that we hope will be the focus for ethics study by school leaders. We feel that if we can write standards that reflect the purpose of supporting the personal growth and development of the leadership capacity of our students, particularly in a world that is not always fair and just, or caring and empathetic, then the risk of misusing such standards is worth it.

ETHICAL DELIBERATION IN THE CLASSROOM

As evident from our students, teaching ethical deliberation has relevance in the classroom. Over the years, we have had many classroom teachers in our administrative preparation programs who have commented about the relevance and application of democratic ethics in their classroom settings. Recall Dewey's admonition that democracy is the place where the group's responsibility is to maximize the potential of each of its individuals, and the individual's responsibility is to support the group in this process. This can be translated into classroom teaching in several ways.

First, one can see this way of thinking in how boundaries and rules are established in the classroom. Traditional classroom management requires that children accept the educational process as something imposed from authority on high. We recall a sign in a classroom stating, "Rule Number 1: The teacher is always right. Rule Number 2: If the teacher is wrong, refer to Rule Number 1." The humor of the sign masks the assumption that classroom management means absolute control. Expected to control, teachers are not encouraged to shape the democratic skills that their children need in an increasingly diverse society.

An alternative approach is to establish rules and boundaries in collaboration with the children. Teachers can assist their students in understanding the objectives that bring them to the classroom in the first place. Involving them in the process is a way to encourage participation in classroom rule making and foster understanding that people establish laws for the purpose of accomplishing tasks that are desirable. In ethical language, this is about the duties as well as desires that make for living cooperatively together. We believe that active engagement underscores the building of democratic ethics where there is group as well as individual responsibility. This translates directly into engaged citizenry as children mature into adults participating in a democratic society.

Democratic ethics can help a class of students, no matter how young, come to understand the desirability of being supportive of each other's learning. This does not mean that the classroom is devoid of behavioral flare-ups. That would be unrealistic. But it offers the teacher and the children a metaethic for understanding that we all have duties, desires, virtues, and values, and that there are consequences that go along with actions taken. Such understanding, we believe, will help to shape a much better equipped citizenry for the responsibilities of adulthood.

TEACHING AND MODELING DEMOCRATIC LEADERSHIP

We want to underscore our belief that prospective and practicing educational leaders need to teach and model democratic leadership in their school communities. In earlier chapters, we discussed how an inquiry method such as the DIRR method could build the democratic moral capacity of a school over time. But school leaders need to take responsibility for helping others understand and apply the method. This means that time must be spent in establishing the rules and boundaries that a method such as DIRR requires. The leader must learn to put away ego and model the listening that goes into all good communication. There also needs to be conscious cultural shaping that reinforces the behaviors of your teachers, parents, and other participants as you take up ethical deliberation.

In essence, we are advocating the need to teach and model democratic leadership, not by telling others what to do but by teaching and facilitating. More than ever, we see that school leaders need to actively listen to and honor varied perspectives. Leaders need to be able to negotiate the individual differences toward common goals and objectives that benefit the school community. Rather than being the only leader, they can develop leadership by encouraging the involvement and participation of school members. These include those in the wider community as well as those members affiliated directly with the school. We tend not to train leaders this way. Our popular culture still admires the solo heroic leader, and the narratives of effective leadership that are most available to us identify these representations. But there are other models of leadership that foster caring, compassion, and inclusion starting from within the educational setting and extending into the community at large.

CONCLUDING THOUGHTS

Our focus in this concluding chapter was on the "how" and "where" of teaching ethics. We presented our own teaching approaches but also suggested that ethical deliberation needs to be considered in other venues. We proposed that applied ethics can be integrated in classroom teaching through collaboration and shared decision making. We extended this to the role of school administrator and specified how democratic ethics is viable as a framework for a different kind of leadership.

We find ourselves asking if, during the current context of standards and accountability, there is room for what Heslep (1997) calls a philosophical model of leadership, with inquiry and philosophical values at the core of leadership decision making. Accountability is about making decisions that produce right actions and good outcomes. As all decisions have ethical implications, the study of ethics and ethical deliberation is central to the ability to truly reform education. We hope the foundations, methods, and applications provided in this book serve to encourage your understanding of the subject. As well, we hope that you will find a way to frame your own leadership in terms that will produce truly meaningful change in educating our children.

NOTE

1. Portions of this chapter are from an earlier paper presented by the authors together with R. C. Paull at the American Educational Research Association annual meeting in 2002.

References

Armstrong, K. (2001). *Buddha.* New York: Penguin.

Athenassoulis, N. (2004). Virtue ethics. In *The Internet encyclopedia of philosophy.* Retrieved November 1, 2004, from www.iep.utm.edu/v/virtue.htm#SH2a.

Augustine, St. (1963). *Confessions* (R. Warner, Trans.). New York: Mentor-Omega.

Badaracco, J. L., Jr. (2006). *Questions of character: Illuminating the heart of leadership through literature.* Boston: Harvard Business School.

Beck, L. (1994). *Reclaiming educational administration as a caring profession.* New York: Teachers College, Columbia University.

Beck, L., & Murphy, J. (1994). *Ethics in educational leadership programs: An expanding role.* Thousand Oaks, CA: Corwin.

Belenky, M. F., Clinchy, B. M., Goldberger, N. R., & Tarule, J. M. (1986). *Women's ways of knowing: Development of self, voice, and mind.* New York: Basic Books.

Bilimoria, P. (1991). Indian ethics. In P. Singer (Ed.), *A companion to ethics* (pp. 43–57). Malden, MA: Blackwell.

Brown, J. F. (1909). *The American high school.* Norwood, MA: J. S. Cushing/Berwick & Smith.

Buckle, S. (1991). Natural law. In P. Singer (Ed.), *A companion to ethics* (pp. 161–174). Malden, MA: Blackwell.

Conley, S., & Enomoto, E. (2005). Routines in school organizations: Creating stability and change. *Journal of Educational Administration, 43*(1), 9–21.

Council of Chief State School Officers. (2001). *ISLLC standards.* Retrieved July 14, 2006, from www.ccsso.org/standards.html.

Delmar, R. (2001). What is feminism? In A. C. Herrmann & A. J. Stewart (Eds.), *Theorizing feminism: Parallel trends in the humanities and social sciences* (2nd ed., pp. 5–28). Boulder, CO: Westview.

Dewey, J. (1916). *Middle works: Volume 9. Democracy and education.* In L. Hickman (Ed.), *The collected works of John Dewey, 1882–1953: Electronic edition.* Carbondale, IL: The Center for Dewey Studies, 1996.

Dewey, J. (1927). *Later works: Volume 2. The public and its problems.* In L. Hickman (Ed.), *The collected works of John Dewey, 1882–1953: Electronic edition.* Carbondale, IL: The Center for Dewey Studies, 1996.

Dewey, J. (1930). *Later works: Volume 5. Essays: Three independent factors in morals.* In L. Hickman (Ed.), *The collected works of John Dewey, 1882–1953: Electronic edition.* Carbondale, IL: The Center for Dewey Studies, 1996.

Dewey, J. (1934). *A common faith.* New Haven, CT: Yale University.

Dewey, J. (1938). *Later works: Volume 10. Art as experience.* In L. Hickman (Ed.), *The collected works of John Dewey, 1882–1953: Electronic edition.* Carbondale, IL: The Center for Dewey Studies, 1996.

Dewey, J., & Tufts, J. (1932a). *Later Works: Volume 7. Ethics.* In L. Hickman (Ed.), *The collected works of John Dewey, 1882–1953: Electronic edition.* Carbondale, IL: The Center for Dewey Studies, 1996.

Dewey, J., & Tufts, J. H. (1932b). *Moral education* (Rev. ed.). New York: Henry Holt & Sons.

Enomoto, E. K. (1997). Negotiating the ethics of care and justice. *Educational Administration Quarterly, 33*(3), 351–370.

Fasching, D. J., & deChant, D. (2001). *Comparative religious ethics: A narrative approach.* Malden, MA: Blackwell.

Feldman, M. S. (1988). *Understanding organizational routines.* Bergen, Norway: Norwegian Research Center for Organization and Management, University of Bergen.

Ferguson, K. E. (1984). *The feminist case against bureaucracy.* Philadelphia: Temple University.

Fesmire, S. (2003). *John Dewey and moral imagination.* Bloomington, IN: Indiana University.

Frankena, W. K. (1963). *Ethics.* Englewood Cliffs, NJ: Prentice-Hall.

Fullan, M. (2003). *The moral imperative of school leadership.* Thousand Oaks, CA: Corwin.

Gilligan, C. (1982). *In a different voice: Psychological theory and women's development.* Cambridge, MA: Harvard University.

Green, R. (1988). *Religion and moral reason.* Oxford, U.K.: Oxford University.

Greenfield, W. D. (1993). Articulating values and ethics in administrator preparation. In C. Capper (Ed.), *Educational administration in a pluralistic society* (pp. 267–287). Albany, NY: SUNY.

Haldane, J. (1991). Medieval and Renaissance ethics. In P. Singer (Ed.), *A companion to ethics* (pp. 133–146). Malden, MA: Blackwell.

Hare-Mustin, R. T., & Marecek, J. (2001). Gender and the meaning of difference: Postmodernism and psychology. In A. C. Herrmann & A. J. Stewart (Eds.), *Theorizing feminism: Parallel trends in the humanities and social sciences* (2nd ed., pp. 78–109). Boulder, CO: Westview.

Held, V. (1993). *Feminist morality.* Chicago: University of Chicago.

Heslep, R. D. (1997). The practical value of philosophical thought for the ethical dimension of educational leadership. *Educational Administration Quarterly, 33*(1), 67–85.

hooks, b. (1984). *Feminist theory: From margin to center.* Boston: South End.

Houston, B. (1996). Feminism. In J. J. Chambliss (Ed.), *Philosophy of education: An encyclopedia* (pp. 215–220). New York: Garland.

Interstate School Leadership Licensure Consortium (ISLLC). (1996). *Interstate School Leadership Licensure Consortium: Standards for school leaders.* Washington, DC: Council of Chief State School Officers.

Kant, I. (1785). Introduction to metaphysics of morals. Retrieved November 1, 2004, from http://eserver.org/philosophy/kant/intro-to-metaphys-of-morals.txt.

Katz, M. S., Noddings, N., & Strike, K. A. (Eds.). (1999). *Justice and caring: The search for common ground in education.* New York: Teachers College, Columbia University.

Kellner, M. (1991). Jewish ethics. In P. Singer (Ed.), *A companion to ethics* (pp. 82–90). Malden, MA: Blackwell.

Kidder, R. (1995). *How good people make tough choices: Resolving the dilemmas of ethical living.* New York: William Morrow & Company.

Kramer, B. H. (2006a). Democracy and democratic ethics. In F. English (Ed.), *The Sage encyclopedia of educational leadership.* Thousand Oaks, CA: Sage.

Kramer, B. H. (2006b). Ethics. In F. English (Ed.), *The Sage encyclopedia of educational leadership.* Thousand Oaks, CA: Sage.

Kramer, B. H., Paull, R., & Enomoto, E. K. (2002). *Teaching ethics in an era of accountability: Dilemmas and possibilities.* Paper presented at the American Educational Research Association, New Orleans, LA.

Kymlicka, W. (1991). The social contract tradition. In P. Singer (Ed.), *A companion to ethics* (pp. 186–196). Malden, MA: Blackwell.

LaMagdeleine, D. R., & Kramer, B. H. (1998). Transgression and forgiveness in an international school: A nonmodern case study. *Educational Administration Quarterly, 34*(3), 421–455.

MacIntyre, A. (1966). *A short history of ethics.* New York: Macmillan.

MacIntyre, A. (1984). *After virtue* (2nd ed.). Notre Dame, IN: University of Notre Dame.

Marshall, C. (1997). Dismantling and reconstructing policy analysis. In C. Marshall (Ed.), *Feminist critical policy analysis* (Vol. 1). London: Falmer.

Maxcy, S. J. (2002). *Ethical school leadership.* Lanham, MD: Scarecrow.

McCarthy, M. M. (1999). The evolution of educational leadership preparation programs. In J. Murphy & K. Seashore-Louis (Eds.), *Handbook of research on educational administration* (2nd ed.). San Francisco: Jossey-Bass.

Midgley, M. (1991). The origins of ethics. In P. Singer (Ed.), *A companion to ethics* (pp. 3–13). Malden, MA: Blackwell.

Nafisi, A. (2005). Mysterious connections that link us together. Washington, DC: National Public Radio. Retrieved July 22, 2005, from www.npr.org.

Nanji, Azim. (1991). Islamic ethics. In P. Singer (Ed.), *A companion to ethics* (pp. 106–118). Malden, MA: Blackwell.

Noddings, N. (1992). *The challenge to care in schools.* New York: Teachers College, Columbia University.

Noddings, N. (2003). *Caring: A feminine approach to ethics and moral education* (2nd ed.). New York: Teachers College, Columbia University.

O'Neill, O. (1991). Kantian ethics. In P. Singer (Ed.), *A companion to ethics* (pp. 175–185). Malden, MA: Blackwell.

Palmer, P. J. (2004). *A hidden wholeness: The journey toward an undivided life.* San Francisco: Jossey-Bass.

Rawls, J. (1971). *A theory of justice.* Cambridge, MA: Harvard University.

Riehl, C. J. (2000). The principal's role in creating inclusive schools for diverse students: A review of normative, empirical and critical literature on the practice of educational administration. *Review of educational research, 70*(1), 55–81.

Robinson, D., & Garratt, C. (2004). *Introducing ethics.* London: Icon Books.

Rowe, C. (1991). Ethics in ancient Greece. In P. Singer (Ed.), *A companion to ethics* (pp. 121–132). Malden, MA: Blackwell.

Ruether, R. (1992). *Gaia and God: An ecofeminist theology of earth healing.* San Francisco: Harper.

Schneewind, J. B. (1991). Modern moral philosophy. In P. Singer (Ed.), *A companion to ethics* (pp. 147–157). Malden, MA: Blackwell.

Sergiovanni, T. J. (1992). *Moral leadership: Getting to the heart of school improvement.* San Francisco: Jossey-Bass.

Sergiovanni, T. J. (1995). *The principalship: A reflective practice perspective.* San Francisco: Jossey-Bass.

Shapiro, J. P., & Stefkovich, J. A. (2005). *Ethical leadership and decision making in education* (2nd ed.). Mahwah, NJ: Lawrence Erlbaum.

Siegfried, C. H. (1996). *Pragmatism and feminism: Reweaving the social fabric.* Chicago: University of Chicago.

Starratt, R. J. (1994). *Building the ethical school.* New York: Falmer.

Starratt, R. J. (1996). *Transforming educational administration: Meaning, community and excellence.* New York: McGraw-Hill.

Starratt, R. J. (2003). *Centering educational administration: Cultivating meaning, community, responsibility.* Mahwah, NJ: Lawrence Erlbaum.

Starratt, R. J. (2004). *Ethical leadership.* San Francisco: Jossey-Bass.

Strike, K. (2006). *Ethical leadership in schools: Creating community in an environment of accountability.* Thousand Oaks, CA: Corwin.

Strike, K. A., Haller, E. J., & Soltis, J. F. (1998). *The ethics of school administration* (2nd ed.). New York: Teachers College.

Thompson, M. (2003). *Ethics.* London: Hodder Headline.

Vaill, P. B. (1996). *Learning as a way of being: Strategies for survival in a world of permanent white water.* San Francisco: Jossey-Bass.

Van Cleave, M. (1994). *The least of these: Stories of schoolchildren.* Thousand Oaks, CA: Corwin.

Walker, M. U. (1998). *Moral understandings: A feminist study in ethics.* New York: Routledge.

Index

accountability, 13, 133, 140, 143
administrative work, 53, 56, 62
antecedent factors, 12–14, 16, 109
Aquinas, St. Thomas, 6
Aristotle, 4–6, 9, 30–31;
    Nichomachean Ethics, 5

Bentham, Jeremy, 7, 9, 27, 28
book assumptions, xii–xiii, 131
book contents, xii–xiv, xvii–xxi,
    131, 136
book guidelines, xiv
Brown, John Franklin, *The American
    High School*, 61–62
Buddhism, 45–47

cases: academic freedom, 123–25;
    career interference, 127–29;
    choosing a new principal, 111–15;
    homecoming, 120–22; leadership
    award, 125–27; PE exemption,
    115–17; sexual encounter, 117–20
categorical imperative, 8, 24–26
challenges in teaching, 139–40
Christianity, 44–46
conflicting sources of ethical
    tensions, 42

consequential factors, 3, 14–15, 18
consequentialism, 15, 92
Council of Chief State School
    Officers, xvii

defining a useful method, 91–93
democracy, 84
democratic ethics, ix, xviii, xxi, 3,
    17–18, 86, 131, 141, 143
democratic leadership, 4–5, 18,
    53, 69, 73, 76, 79, 81, 82, 87,
    131, 142; conditions, xiv–xix;
    teaching and modeling,
    141–42
deontological ethics, 40
deontology, 9, 18
desires-based ethics, xviii, 19, 22,
    28–29, 36, 40, 136
Dewey, John, 20, 34, 80; art as
    experience, 14; common faith, 42,
    49–51, 53; communication, 84;
    democracy, 73, 80, 83–85;
    democracy and education, 83–85;
    democratic ethics, 19–20; ethics
    of democratic leadership, 73;
    moral imagination, 85, 87, 135.
    See also problems of association

DIRR method, 89–106, 111;
    description, 97–98; interpretation,
    98–100; rediscernment, 102–5,
    rehearsal, 100–102
discernment and action, 93–97
Durkheim, Emile, 43
duties-based ethics, 20, 22–23, 25,
    37
duty, *deon* (Greek), 22
duty, juridical (legal), 23

eco-feminism, 66–69
end, *telos* (Greek), 26
ends-based ethics, 20, 40
ethical deliberation, classroom,
    140–41
ethical dilemma, 15–17
ethical tension, xviii, 17, 19, 26, 38,
    39, 42, 55, 99, 112
ethics: definition of, xii; description
    of, 3–4; *ethike* (Greek), 4; *ethos*
    (Greek), 4

feminism: applied, 58–61; definition
    of, 56–58

gender, xii, 1, 32, 57–61, 63–65
good ends, 3, 6, 10–11, 30–31, 86,
    133–34
good society ethics, 21–22, 32–34
Greek origins, 3

habitual responses, xii–xiii
Hinduism, 46
Hobbes, Thomas, 6
hooks, bell, 65

imperative: categorical, 24;
    hypothetical, 24

individual vs. group needs, 10–11,
    73, 79, 81, 87
Islam, 20, 45, 115
Interstate School Leaders Liscensure
    Consortium (ISLLC), xvii, 140

Judaism, 45
judgments and consequences, 38–40

Kant, Immanuel, 8; *Fundamental
    Principles of Metaphysics of
    Morals*, 23
Kohlberg, Lawrence, moral
    development, 59
Kurosawa, Akira, 89

leadership preparation, xvi, xxi, 140

Marx, Karl, 6, 7, 25
Mill, John Stuart, *On Liberty*, 8
moral imagination, 85–86, 88,
    89–90, 92, 135
moral imperative, xiv–xv
morality, *mos/mores* (Latin), 43
Moulton, John Fletcher, 19

Nafisi, Azar, *Huckleberry Finn*,
    50–51
National Council for Accreditation
    of Teacher Education (NCATE),
    140
National Organization for Women
    (NOW), 57

Palmer, Parker, 67
Plato, 4–6, 30; *The Republic*, 6
problems of association, 76–79;
    change conflicts, 78–79; private
    vs. public, 79; social order, 76–78

Rawls, John, *A Theory of Justice*, 33–34

reflection, xiv, 5, 38, 39, 40, 91, 93, 95, 96, 98, 106, 131, 137, 138, 139

religion: definition of, 42–44; *ligo* (Latin), 42

religion vs. religious attitudes, 49–51

religious freedom, 48–49

religious traditions, 44–48

right action, 9–11, 15

Rousseau, Jean-Jacques, *Emile*, 7

Ruether, Rosemary, 64–65

sacred and holy, 51–52

Sartre, Jean Paul, 9

Socrates, 4, 5, 9

Sophocles, *Antigone*, 39

standards-based education, xiv, 117, 140

Starratt, Robert J.: building the ethical school, 35–36; educational administration, xvi; ethical leader, xvi; ethical leadership, xv; ethical schools, 35

stories: deciding on employee healthcare, 27–28; math-beliefs spectrum, 26; Nancy's dilemma, 73–87; Noni, xi–xii; SPCO's dilemma, 94–97

teaching approaches, similarities and differences, 137–39

teaching narratives, 132–37

teleological system, 26–29

teleological view, 4

Thoreau, Henry David, *Walden*, 7

toward resolution, 105

universal, 20

universalist ethics, 22–26

utilitarian system, 22–26

utilitarianism, 7, 8, 9, 15, 18, 27

virtue, *arete* (Greek), 4

virtue ethics, 20, 30–32

working the dilemma, xiv, 81, 91, 96, 103